D0893543

THE
TALKING
CLOWNS

THE TALKING CLOWNS

FROM LAUREL AND HARDY
TO THE
MARX BROTHERS

BY FRANK MANCHEL

FRANKLIN WATTS   NEW YORK   LONDON   1976

All photographs courtesy of
the Lester Glassner Collection

Designed by Nick Krenitsky

Library of Congress Cataloging in Publication Data

Manchel, Frank
    The talking clowns.

        Bibliography: p.
        Includes index.
        SUMMARY: Brief sketches of the life and
    careers of the great talking film comedians of the
    1930's: Laurel and Hardy, W.C. Fields, Mae West,
    and the Marx Brothers.
        1. Comedians—United States—Biography—
    Juvenile literature. 2. Comedy films — History and
    criticism — Juvenile literature. [1. Comedians. 2.
    Comedy films — History and criticism] I. Title.
    PN1998.A2M277   791.43'028'0922 [B] [920]   75–37902
    ISBN 0–531–01153–4

FOR MY SISTER ROSE

"God bless all clowns
So poor the world would be
Lacking their piquant touch, hilarity,
The belly laughs, the ringing, lovely mirth
That makes a friendly place of this earth."

STAN LAUREL

CONTENTS

THE
TALKING
CLOWNS

INTRODUCTION

THE CLASSIC CLOWNS

Hollywood's famous talking comedians are back on top of the popularity poll. Not since the 1930s have laughmakers such as Stan Laurel, Oliver Hardy, W. C. Fields, Mae West, and the Marx Brothers been so welcomed by audiences around the world.

The revival of interest in early sound comedy has been underscored by the honors being paid its stars. Many books on the lives and art of the first talking clowns have appeared in the last few years. Film festivals devoted to their careers are now commonplace. And, at long last, the Academy of Motion Picture Arts and Sciences has begun to award special Oscars to comedians such as Charles Chaplin and Groucho Marx for their brilliant contributions to film history.

Why this great emphasis now on the great clowns of the 1930s? How do these comics and their movies relate to us?

One purpose of this book is to examine these questions. I assume, first, that comedy is no laughing matter. Not only those who provide the laughs but also those who enjoy them need comedy in their lives. Maybe it is because laughter is society's rarest medicine. It cures our states of depression, eases our tensions, and improves our view of others as well as of ourselves. And no one understands the importance of comedy in our lives better than do the entertainment moguls. To them, comedy is big business. Consider, for example, television. Old movies and comedy shows receive a larger percentage of time on TV than any other category of show. In fact, many of us discovered Chaplin, Laurel and Hardy, Fields, West, and the Marx Brothers on the television screen. Considering its tremendous popularity, when has there ever been a better time to examine the history and relevance of sound comedy?

The American sound comedy film has proven to be one of our most valuable and popular gifts to world culture. Ironically, its birth occurred during one of the most troubled times in American history: the depression years, from 1929 to 1935. These were the days when unemployment reached staggering proportions, when hunger robbed men and women of their pride, and when the young found themselves moving aimlessly across the country.

Although the coming of talking pictures in the late 1920s offered escape to the desperate and disillusioned, it was not the overnight sensation so often reported. Almost seven years passed before

3

most movie houses found the need and money to renovate their silent film equipment. The major studios, for their part, moved cautiously in adapting to the sound revolution. Their major concessions, at first, were talking short subjects and musical revues. Such ventures hardly appealed to the great clowns of the day. Charles Chaplin, Buster Keaton, Harold Lloyd, and Harry Langdon continued making silent pictures. These kings of comedy ignored the signs and, except for Chaplin, soon passed from the scene.

Because there is some confusion about Chaplin's role in sound comedy, it's worthwhile discussing his later career now. Although he remained a great comedian, he was not a major figure in screen comedy after the 1920s. For that reason Chaplin is not treated separately in this book. In the 1930s, when the film industry was turned upside down, Chaplin made only two films—*City Lights* (1931) and *Modern Times* (1936)—and both were basically silent movies with musical sound tracks. Although it was clear he had lost none of his talent, it was also clear Chaplin did not want to make talking films. But he could not hold out forever. In *The Great Dictator* (1940), audiences for the first time heard and saw a new Chaplin. He was still funny and beautiful to watch, yet something was missing. His dialogue seemed strained. Critics and fans expressed disappointment over his sound techniques. These complaints, plus the public's disapproval of Chaplin's "subversive" political views and private life, discouraged the great clown. He incorporated his feelings into his next two films, *Monsieur Verdoux* (1947) and *Limelight* (1952), both of which met with a poor reception at the box office. The crushing blow to his career came in September 1952 when anti-Communist "witchhunts" were a commonplace. While Chaplin was traveling with his family to England to attend the British premiere of *Limelight*, the United States government revoked his reentry permit (he had never become an American citizen). Rather than submit to the cowardly and unfair persecution of then Attorney General James McGranery, the Chaplins took up residence in Switzerland. After that, the brilliant clown made only two more films—A *King in New York* (1957) and A *Countess from Hong Kong* (1967)—both of which were artistic and commercial failures. Happily, the story does not end on a sad note. Chaplin, after a twenty-year absence, made a

4

triumphant return to America, where on April 11, 1972, he received a special Oscar from a cheering and grateful Motion Picture Academy. Three years later, on March 4, the frail eighty-five-year-old genius was dubbed Sir Charles Chaplin by Queen Elizabeth II in the ornate ballroom of Buckingham Palace—three miles from the slums where he had grown up in poverty.

Because Chaplin and the other great silent clowns did not fit into the new age of talking films, Hollywood began a search for more adaptable comedians. The word also went out for playwrights and poets, novelists and stage directors, to come to California to contribute their talents to the talkies.

The main purpose of this book is to pay an affectionate visit— the text is too short to do otherwise—with those who became the great talking comedians and created memorable sound comedy films. Clearly, it is not enough to discuss the films unless we also reveal something about the personalities who made the comedies what they were. My one regret is that not everyone who deserves a share in the spotlight can get it here. Hopefully, you will want to read more about the talking clowns.

In the meantime, I am thankful for this chance to reminisce about some of the most marvelous show people ever to come out of Hollywood.

THE IMMORTAL BRATS

STAN LAUREL
AND
OLIVER HARDY

Everyone remembers reading about the important discovery the public made in 1927 when it flocked to see the revolutionary movie *The Jazz Singer,* in which Al Jolson actually talked, sang, and joked. Even if the motion picture industry didn't realize what was going on, the viewers knew that the silent film days were gone forever. But few readers remember that the public also made another important discovery in 1927, one that brought together the most beloved comedy team in all of film history: Stan Laurel and Oliver Hardy.

Stan acted the part of the thin, sensitive underdog with a fool's mind who, faced with a problem, scratched his head in wonder and cried out of embarrassment. Ollie, fat, fussy, and short-tempered, also played an underdog; but, unlike Laurel, Hardy never doubted his ability to master any problem. The fact that his misplaced confidence only made matters worse failed to impress him. Furthermore, he always made it a point of staring at the camera to show his disbelief, not only at Stan's stupidity, but also at the fact that they always wound up in such outrageous situations.

Stan and Ollie, however, were no ordinary, harmless screen simpletons. Far from it! In their grown-up bodies were immature minds, which reasoned foolishly that anyone who offended their childlike dignity must be punished . . . and punished severely. The smallest insult gave Laurel and Hardy the spark to destroy their enemy. And they did . . . slowly, calmly, and with increasing scope. Perhaps, as George Orwell explained, it was this aspect of their comedy that made the team so appealing; they represented ". . . a less responsible man who is inside all of us, can never be suppressed altogether, and needs a hearing occasionally."

Starting in 1927, Laurel and Hardy, over the next eighteen years, appeared in a number of memorable silent and sound comedy shorts, as well as in a few outstanding feature films. Taken together, their movies prove that of all the silent clowns, these two unusual men made the move to talking films better than anyone else. But they did not become stars overnight, they did not break into films as a team, and they were not new to film-making in 1927. What's more, Laurel and Hardy paired up by accident and needed help in forming their screen images from the one man in Hollywood who, in the late 1920s, ran the best fun factory anywhere: Hal Roach.

By 1925, Roach's reputation as a comedy executive rated pretty high in the film capital of the world, and why not? He had helped develop such great screen comedians as Harold Lloyd, Will Rogers, the *Our Gang* crew, Edgar Kennedy, Snub Pollard, Charley Chase, and Thelma Todd. In addition, Roach had improved on the great Mack Sennett's slapstick formulas.

Sennett stressed the supremacy of gags in comedy films, downgrading stars, story material, and reality. His movies portrayed a mad world, where no sane person ever lived. Roach, on the other hand, made comedies involving believable people in familiar situations which suddenly turned into nightmares. Only then did mayhem erupt. The comedy relied on the audience identifying with the comedian's problems. "They were funny," said Roach explaining the appeal of his characters, "because you have seen but not really recognized them [in] yourself." Of course, we "knew" that none of us were as ridiculous as Laurel and Hardy, but, so our egos told us, many of our friends and associates fitted the bill nicely. Thus, Roach comedies gave us the chance to laugh at our peers without hurting our day-to-day relationships.

His method of making comedy movies was not much different from that of other fun houses of the time. The idea for a film was presented first to Roach, who then added some touches of his own before passing on the suggestion to his gag writers and directors. Once a suitable outline had been prepared, a cast and crew were assembled and production started. No one ever knew from that moment on what would come next. Each scene got rehearsed, tested, shot, and reviewed, with everyone from stagehand to star voicing his views on what worked. Even when the crew agreed, the problem wasn't settled. To ensure that the average comedy two-reeler had the required seventy-five laughs, the film's gags were tried out in preview screenings. People actually counted the laughs the short received. "That's what they call 'clocking' a comedy," explained one film reviewer. "If it clocks less than that, something is wrong." By such methods, Roach turned out a good comedy short every seven days.

Fortunately for him and film history, Hal Roach had assembled not only a first-rate set of comics but also some outstanding screenwriters, cameramen, and directors. One writer-director was Leo Mc-

Stan Laurel, the thin, sensitive underdog,
in a pose from *Babes in Toyland* (1934).

Oliver Hardy, the fat, fussy clown,
in *Babes in Toyland* (1934).

10

Carey, who in later years gained fame for such movies as *Duck Soup* (1933), *Ruggles of Red Gap* (1935), *Going My Way* (1944) and *An Affair to Remember* (1957). The other soon-to-be-famous talent was George Stevens, whose skill later created such motion pictures as *Gunga Din* (1939), *Woman of the Year* (1941), *A Place in the Sun* (1951), *Shane* (1953), *Giant* (1956), and *The Diary of Anne Frank* (1959). But in 1925, Roach felt that the studio needed a lift. What he had been doing was fine, but not very special. Like most comedy people, Roach searched for the unusual and thus decided to gamble on a hunch.

Believing erroneously that the public paid only to see big names, he brought together a number of fading movies stars such as Mabel Normand, Theda Bara, and Lionel Barrymore and featured them in a new series entitled "All-Star Comedies." The idea flopped, but the series itself provided the turning point for two of the studio's supporting comics.

One was Stan Laurel, born Arthur Stanley Jefferson in Ulverston, Lancashire, England, on June 16, 1890. His father was a well-known theatrical manager who also wrote for and acted on the stage. As a result, Stan dreamed of being like his father, although the son didn't make his stage debut until he had passed his sixteenth birthday. By then, most of his life had been spent backstage, studying the various acts and routines, learning the basics of popular entertainment.

In 1910, Stan got his first big break. He joined the Fred Karno Pantomime Company, one of the most important comedy groups at the turn of the century. Here was the best school for acquiring the art of split-second timing, mimicry, and burlesque. What's more, Stan shared his apprenticeship with another youngster named Charles Chaplin. The two budding clowns roomed together and enjoyed each other's company, although once Charles became a screen star their relationship ended.

The Karno years were important ones for both boys, but their apprenticeship came to a halt in 1913 when the troupe was on tour in America and Chaplin quit to work in Sennett films. This ruined Karno's chances for good future billings and the company soon disbanded, leaving each performer to his own devices. The talented Stanley Jefferson changed his name to Stan Laurel, became a knock-

11

Stan and Ollie with Hal Roach, producer, sometimes writer and director, and the man who started the team of Laurel and Hardy.

about comic in vaudeville, and discovered to his delight that audiences loved his frequent imitations of Chaplin, who, by mid-1914, had already become a popular film clown.

Despite his obvious interest in movie comedy, Stan didn't try his hand at films until 1917, and then proved so insignificant that within a few months he was back doing live shows. Interestingly, it was during one of those vaudeville tours that he caught the eye of a small film producer who hired him to appear in a comedy movie in which Stan gets robbed by the company's comic villain, Oliver Hardy. Afterward, Stan went back to vaudeville, while Oliver continued to work for the company.

For Hardy, the road to the movies had been very different from Laurel's. Born Norvell Hardy on January 18, 1892, in Harlem,

Stan as the dim-witted Scotsman who is too shy to be examined
by the ship's doctor (Sam Lufkin) in *Putting Pants on Philip*.
Although made in 1926, the film was not released until the following year,
when Laurel and Hardy first started to become popular.

Georgia, he was the youngest of five children in a family that had no
ties at all with show business. Oliver Hardy, the father, was a lawyer
who died young. After her husband's death, the mother moved the
three boys and two girls to Milledgeville, Georgia, where she sup-
ported herself by running a hotel. Unlike Stan, Norvell went regularly to school and grew up in a rather traditional way. The boy's only
apparent interest in theatrics came through his love for music, and
he often took singing lessons to improve his voice. Norvell, like
Laurel, was influenced by his father and tried to pursue a career in
law, but found in 1910 that operating a local movie house was much
more fun. Three years later, he lost interest in the house but not
in the movies and went to Jacksonville, Florida, to try his luck at film
acting. For five dollars a day, he put his huge bulk to work as a

clown and "heavy" foil to the comic leads and proved quite good at it.

When not playing "bad guy" roles, "Babe," as he was now affectionately known, began developing a comic image patterned after a popular Georgia comic-strip character named "Helpful Henry." Henry, fat, fussy, and pompous, never seemed to do anything right. His one saving grace was his "heart of gold." Although it would be more than a decade before Hardy perfected this screen image, it was the basic role that his future fame rested on.

The Florida company that Babe worked for was the same one that in 1917 hired Laurel to appear as a victim in the two-reeler *Lucky Dog*. It was the only time the two clowns worked together until 1926, when they met again at the Roach studio.

Over that nine-year period, the boys presented quite different attitudes toward their work and future. Stan, for example, tried to establish himself on screen first as a vicious simpleton, noted for speed, a quick temper, and ridiculous behavior. In short, a totally unsympathetic and typical slapstick comic of the silent cinema. Realizing the drawbacks, Laurel worked just as hard at earning a reputation as a good gag man and an adequate director. His writing efforts paid off when Roach hired him in the mid-twenties to work full time as a gag man at the studio. Oliver "Babe" Hardy, as he started billing himself in 1918, concentrated instead on his visual comedy, taking advantage of the silent audience's interest in big, fat villains who acted as perfect heavies for the top comedians. His reputation grew over the next decade, particularly in his two-reelers with Larry Semon, the white-faced little clown who, in the 1920s, rivaled the kings of silent comedy themselves. (Ironically, Laurel had also worked with Semon, but the two never got along and the relationship only added to Stan's mistaken belief that his future lay behind, rather than in front of, the camera.) By 1926, Hardy had made his way to Roach's fun factory, but mainly as a comic villain. Thus, as the last days of the silent film were fast approaching, the two men destined to become the first great talking clowns were working for Hollywood's best comedy producer, but in roles totally different from the ones that turned them into famous stars.

And then fate stepped in. Laurel got the directing and gag-writing chores for the All-Star comedy *Get 'Em Young*, in which Hardy played the butler. But before the filming had gone very far, Oliver burned his hand while on the set and was forced to leave the film. Having no one readily available to replace Hardy, Stan took over the role and proved funny enough to have Roach insist that Laurel once more become a clown and write himself into the next film, *Slipping Wives*. Roach also made a point of praising Stan for his impromptu bit in *Get 'Em Young* when the skinny comic, frightened, suddenly wrinkled his face and began to cry. Stan didn't particularly like the gag, but for the rest of his career it remained a fixture in his screen image.

Slipping Wives had Laurel and Hardy appearing in the same film for the second time in their lives, again, not as a team, but as two supporting comics. From then on, one rarely appeared without the other, although it took months before Roach realized what a gold mine he had. The boys themselves worked on their comedy roles individually, with no thought given to the other clown. In the meantime, *Slipping Wives* was released in April 1927 and, by the time *The Jazz Singer* appeared a few months later, exhibitors and distributors reported a growing interest in the fat and the skinny comics appearing regularly in the new Roach two-reelers.

Working on his intuition, Roach turned the boys over to his writers with instructions to team them up in what is generally regarded as the first "official" Laurel and Hardy comedy, *Putting Pants on Philip*.

Although released in 1927, the film was made the year before and kept off the market until the boys were better known. The plot focused on a shy but sex-minded Scotsman (Laurel) who emigrates to the United States and gets "Americanized" by his pompous uncle (Hardy). In many respects *Putting Pants on Philip* was the standard high-caliber Roach comedy. The gags came off well, while the emphasis remained on strong story construction. The boys themselves performed admirably, but as yet there was no attempt to integrate their roles. Each appeared as an individual, a comedian doing his bit, rather than as a team tied to each other in thought and deed.

One indication, however, of the future direction that Laurel and Hardy comedies would take surfaced in the elements of "homosexual" humor in *Putting Pants on Philip*. That is not to say that their gags were obscene or tasteless. It is to say that Stan and Oliver in this and their later films rarely express love or affection for anyone but each other. What's more, women in their movies almost always are seen as money-hungry parasites who are out to get whatever they can and then leave; or as nagging, bullying, penny-pinching wives who do all in their power to make life miserable for their poor husbands. The fact that this one-sided, negative image of women proved to be almost a standard gag for close to twenty years in Laurel and Hardy movies explains why many women resent these comedians more than any other clowns in movie history. They view the boys as a threat. "With their disaster-prone bodies and their exclusive relationship that not only shuts out women but questions their very necessity," wrote film critic Molly Haskell, "they constitute a two-man wrecking team of female—that is, civilized and bourgeois—society." She goes on to say, "The male duo, from Laurel and Hardy to Abbott and Costello, is almost by definition, or by metaphor, latently homosexual; a union of opposites (tall/short, thin/fat, straight/comic) who, like husband and wife, combine to make a whole."

A second indication from *Putting Pants on Philip* of what Laurel and Hardy fans could expect from future films is the influence that Roach's brand of comedy had on the two clowns who by 1926 were both in their late thirties. Beginning with the producer's basic premise that great comedians imitate children unable to adjust sanely to adult situations, Stan and Ollie acted the parts of immature people whose ineptness leads to disaster. Or, as one critic put it, "Stan and Ollie . . . [represent] naughty children in a world they mistakenly think they can outbully and outshove." Essential to these comic roles is the mistaken idea held by many naïve people that politeness, sincerity, and the appeal to reason are guarantees that in this "ordered" world things will turn out for the best. It just isn't so.

But in 1926–27 these Laurel and Hardy screen conventions were only hinted at. It took many months and hard work before they were perfected. For the next two years the creative clowns, along with Hal Roach, Leo McCarey, George Stevens, and the rest of the studio experts, tried, tested, and improved the "brat" imagery. It's revealing to read the opinions of the key figures themselves as to who was

Stan and Ollie with James Finlayson in a scene
from *Big Business* (1929), a two-reeler considered by many experts
as one of the funniest shorts in the history of motion pictures.

the guiding hand. Roach, for example, recalled that "Laurel and
Hardy used to work on gags in the morning and we'd shoot in the
same afternoon. Hardy was a big, fat, happy-go-lucky chap, always
on time, with the same squawks as any actor, but no more. Laurel
was a great gag man, but lousy with story construction." Hardy, on
the other hand, insists that the team was more interested "in human
appeal" than in "straight comedy." What's more, as their official
biographer John McCabe explained, "Babe always felt that Stan was
the brains and the comedian of the team, and that he was only the
fall guy—the straight man for Stan—a small cog in the wheel." Laurel
himself always credited the working conditions as the basic success
factor. "Sometimes we would be on a gag and it wouldn't work out,"
Stan explained to one interviewer, "so we'd have to wait a couple of

Stan and Ollie in a scene from *The Music Box* (1932),
their only Academy Award–winning film
and one of the best edited of all Laurel and Hardy movies.

days to have the set rebuilt. Things like that mean delay. We never had a regular schedule, but just worked to get a good picture. The studio didn't mind because in those days the salaries weren't worth much money, there weren't any unions, and we never used a big cast." Whoever deserved the credit, and there is no question that everyone played a significant role, the results were wonderful.

By the time the team played a small part in a talking musical review in 1929 they had made some superb silent comedy shorts, the most famous of which were *The Second Hundred Years* (1927), *The Battle of the Century* (1927), and *Two Tars* (1928).

Most fans, however, still favor *Big Business* (1929), which was supervised and written by McCarey, photographed by Stevens, and directed by James W. Horne, with a healthy assist in all categories

18

from Stan Laurel. It remains a perfect example of the team's famous technique of "reciprocal destruction." It is also an excellent showcase for Jimmy Finlayson, their unforgettable sidekick whose quick temper and squinty eyes provided the ideal excuse for chaos.

As always, the story begins in a simple, harmless way. Stan and Ollie appear on the scene as two door-to-door salesmen selling Christmas trees in sunny California during July. Having no success at first, Ollie decides to demonstrate his hard-sell approach. "It's personality that wins," he smugly explains. Then the boys encounter the quick-tempered Finlayson. He, of course, refuses to buy a tree, but when Finn shuts the door, the tree gets caught, and "the gag within a gag" method is put in motion. Every time Ollie rings the bell to free the tree, Stan's coat gets caught, or the tree gets caught again. Finally, on the fourth buzz, Finn angrily throws the tree on the lawn. "I don't think he wants a tree," surmises Ollie. Stan smiles and says, "I've got a big business idea," and then proceeds to ring the bell for the fifth time. When Finn appears, Stan asks, "Could I take your order for next year?" Finn looks at him and tells him to wait a minute so he can get something from inside the house. Stan is thrilled, shouting, "I've got a sale." But his expression changes when Finn reappears with garden shears and cuts the tree up. Stan and Ollie look at each other, then remove their gloves, signaling this is war. The "tit for tat" battle begins slowly. Stan carves up Finn's front door, and Ollie pulls the amazed man's ear. So Finn calmly removes Hardy's watch, evaluates it, and then smashes it on the ground. Before long, the boys have wrecked Finn's lawn and home, as the delirious Finn destroys their car piece by piece. The neighbors, and even a policeman, stand by and watch the goings-on in utter amazement. After total destruction has taken place, the policeman steps in and asks, "Who started all this?" Stan begins to cry, Ollie weeps and fiddles with his tie, and soon everyone is in tears. As a peace gesture, Stan gives Finn a cigar, and sensing that they are safe, the boys wink at each other and start running away, just before the cigar explodes.

No words can adequately describe the film's expert timing, the care given to detail and story construction, let alone the brilliant pantomime performed by Laurel, Hardy, and Finlayson. The laugh-getting gags alone remain some of the best in all of film comedy.

And while we clearly see that Stan and Ollie are spiteful, nasty, and inept "brats," we also see that the people they come in contact with aren't much better.

By 1929, despite the fact that film critics didn't think much of the team, Laurel and Hardy were big box-office hits. Together with McCarey, Stevens, and their favorite director, James Parrott (the real name of the first-rate comedian Charlie Chase), Stan and Ollie moved into sound comedy. They did so without fear or reservations and with a true understanding of what talkies were all about. As Stan explained, "We had decided we weren't talking comedians and of course preferred to do pantomime, like in our silents. So we said as little as possible—only what was necessary to motivate the things we were doing. If there was any plot to be told, we generally would have somebody else tell it. We used sound chiefly for the effects, and after a while we really liked sound, because it emphasized the gags, and, as time went on, we became a little more accustomed, and did more talking than we first intended." Laurel's modesty understates just how creatively the team used sound. First and foremost, they understood that knockabout humor is funnier when the audience doesn't fear for the performer's safety. As a result, their screen violence usually took place outside the camera range, with sound effects punctuating the action. And secondly, they magnified sounds to heighten the dangers and trouble they faced, thereby suggesting that a simple fall was an earth-shattering experience.

The sound shorts they made between 1929 and 1935 in many cases set the standards by which sound comedy came to be judged. Among their best were such films as *Brats* (1930), *Hog Wild* (1930), *Laughing Gravy* (1931), *Helpmates* (1931), *Busy Bodies* (1933), *Them Thar Hills* (1934), and *Tit for Tat* (1935). But no sound short they ever did surpassed *The Music Box* (1932), the only Laurel and Hardy movie ever to receive an Academy Award.

As usual, a simple situation set the gags in motion. The film begins with the caption "Mr. Laurel and Mr. Hardy decided to re-organize and re-supervise their entire financial structure—so they took the $3.80 and went into business." The first job the boys get is to deliver a piano to a house which, unfortunately for them, seems approachable only by means of climbing a long flight of steps. The bossy Hardy is convinced that he can manage the problem, and what follows is an epic struggle to do the absurd. In the midst of their troubles, the boys meet a small number of pompous, petty, and annoying individuals, none of whom has any desire to make things easier for the inept delivery men. One of the film's best moments comes when the boys finally get the piano to the house and learn from the postman that the right way to come is by a back road. Ollie's response is "Why didn't we think of that before?" And so they take the piano all the way back down the steps and bring it the "correct" way. Only then do they discover that no one is home. Stan is willing to give up, but not the smug Ollie. "Where there's a will," he says, "there's a way." And the way for them is to get the piano through a second-story window and then down the staircase and into the living room. You can imagine what follows, but in the midst of their insanity the boys worry most about keeping their hats on their heads. Once the piano is delivered, Stan and Ollie give one of their magnificent impromptu musical interludes, showing their grace and charm as dancers. The end comes, however, when the owner (played by the delightful comic Billy Gilbert) chases them from the house they have wrecked.

Here again Laurel and Hardy show what careful editing around a central idea can do for great comedy. Their feel for rhythm and structure, their ability to build from a simple gag to a complex routine, had by now become exact.

Fate, however, once more intervened. Ever since 1929 Roach had been distributing his films through the Metro-Goldwyn-Mayer organization, and in 1931 the giant studio felt the time had come for the boys to make feature-length talking films. This decision created a problem for the team, who felt that big productions were not suitable for their brand of comedy. (Interestingly, Chaplin, who by now ran his own operation through United Artists, released in 1931 his feature film masterpiece, *City Lights*, a tender love story of a tramp and a blind girl. But the significant point was that it was a silent movie, with a musical score.) Roach, who once argued that brevity was essential to slapstick comedy, now was forced to side with M-G-M. No doubt he was influenced by the growing threat to his two-reelers brought on by sound cartoons called "Silly Symphonies," which featured a comic character named "Mickey Mouse." With M-G-M and Roach in agreement, the team had no choice.

Stan and Ollie with Mae Busch in *Sons of the Desert* (1934),
the best and most clever comedy of their feature film output.

22

Good as they were, they were employees. Laurel never got over the switch to feature films. "We should have stayed in the short-film category," he said years after. "There is just so much comedy one can do along a certain line and then it gets to be unfunny. . . . We didn't want to do feature films in the first place, and even though I've got some favorites among them, I'm sorry we ever did go beyond the two and three reelers."

The controversy still rages among Laurel and Hardy fans over the team's feature films. One side argues that the new working conditions forced upon the comics by M-G-M's mass production policies, as well as the departure of Stevens and McCarey from Roach's studio, set in motion the decline of Laurel and Hardy. Another side argues that the team's decision to make feature films strained their talents, and that after 1932 the quality of their films went downhill. Still another side stresses that they made several good feature films —e.g., *Sons of the Desert* (1934), *Our Relations* (1936), *Way Out West* (1936)—and just became outdated by the end of the decade, mainly because so much of their sound material was a repeat of their silent film shorts. No doubt there is an element of truth in each argument. One thing is certain, however: their fourth feature film, *Sons of the Desert*, remains one of the best comedy films in motion picture history, despite the studio conditions, the familiar gags, and the absence of McCarey, Stevens, and Parrott.

The opening sequence perfectly combines their use of silent and sound film techniques. A secret meeting of the Sons of the Desert, a fraternal club, is under way when Stan and Ollie arrive late and try to find their seats, annoying the members and disrupting the proceedings. The Exalted Ruler is finally allowed to continue his speech, in which he tells the group that they must all attend the national convention, a free swinging affair, in Chicago. "The strong," he says, "must help the weak"; at which point Ollie looks at Stan. Everyone rises to pledge his attendance except Stan, who by now is near tears, frightened that his wife won't let him go. Ollie reassures him it will be no problem, never doubting his own skill in getting his wife's permission to go. So Stan says, "Me too!" and the members end their meeting by singing their alma mater. (Almost all of the scene is in pantomime.)

Laurel and Hardy sharing a laugh with Charlie Chase
in another scene from *Sons of the Desert*.

Being the typical Laurel and Hardy wives, the women refuse to let their husbands go to Chicago, but the boys pull a fast one. Hardy pretends that he's ill, while Laurel brings back a horse doctor who tells Ollie's wife that Hardy needs a Honolulu ocean voyage for his health. Mrs. Hardy insists that her husband go, and he looks at Stan and says, "If I'm going to Honolulu alone, he's going with me."

Everything seems to be going well for the men. They arrive in Chicago, have a wild time, and take part in the giant convention parade. But unknown to them, the ocean liner they supposedly are on runs into trouble at sea, and all the passengers need to be rescued and brought back by a special liner. The duped wives, to take their minds off their anxiety, go to the movies, where to their surprise they see pictures of their husbands clowning at the Sons of the Desert convention.

When the boys return they discover their dilemma and, of course, Hardy exclaims to Laurel, "Nice little mess you've gotten me into." The eventual face-to-face meeting between the couples finally occurs, with the wives betting on which of the husbands is more honest. The women cross-examine the men as if they were naughty children caught in a lie. Soon Stan breaks down and cries, while Ollie twiddles his fingers. In the end, Laurel comes clean and his wife rewards him. Hardy, on the other hand, is punished by his vengeful spouse.

The film has all the features of the great comedy shorts, including excellent pacing, careful cutting, good action sequences, an effective sound track, and superb acting. It shows wonderfully well the by now familiar world of Laurel and Hardy, where inept men struggle to preserve their self-respect, while at the same time trying to enjoy life.

Following 1934, the team had fewer and fewer successes; and after 1940 they left Roach, only to drift in motion pictures from one bad project to another. Finally, in 1945, they quit the business and went into retirement. Fortunately for us and for them, the story didn't end sadly. Starting in the 1950s, their old films began appearing regularly on television and a whole new generation rediscovered Laurel and Hardy. Tributes once more poured in from all over the world, and everywhere millions of people laughed at the immature clowns who were too stupid or too innocent to understand that the meek don't always inherit the earth. Plans were made to star the team in their own television show, but illness stopped the project.

On August 7, 1957, Oliver Hardy died. Almost eight years later, on February 23, 1965, Stan Laurel joined him. Before his death, however, Stan took great satisfaction in seeing the formation of an organization dedicated to the team's memory. Justly called the Sons of the Desert, its members stay in touch with each other on a regular basis, with a national headquarters in New York City. But they always keep in mind Laurel's warning: "Don't sit around and tear comedy apart. It is like a fine watch, and you'll never get it together again. And don't ask me why people laugh—that is the mystery of it all."

THE NOBLEST FRAUD

W. C. FIELDS

No one hates convention more than the Hollywood clown. It's the cornerstone on which his film comedy is built. Starting in America's first decade of moving pictures with John Bunny and running through the works of such great clowns as Charles Chaplin, Buster Keaton, Harold Lloyd, Harry Langdon, Stan Laurel and Oliver Hardy, the Marx Brothers, Mae West, Jerry Lewis, and Woody Allen, the outstanding American comedians roast anyone who takes himself too seriously. And throughout the entire eighty years of this superb tradition, the amazing W. C. Fields emerges at *the* clown who was the most savage in his attack on society's pretensions.

What makes him so amazing is that he made it to the top by breaking every rule in the book. Film producers, in particular, endured more than their share of his methods. Legend has it that one producer refused to rehire Fields, even if the star gave him five million dollars. The person who heard the remark felt the price was too low. Still another source reports that Fields made it a practice "to break as many rules as possible and cause the maximum amount of trouble for everybody." Those viewing his films for the first time are surprised that the movies lack so many "successful" box-office ingredients. There are no gorgeous girls, no erotic love scenes, no breath-taking photography, and no unusual sets. Furthermore, his film plots focus on inept heroes who cheat, drink, lie, and avoid work whenever possible.

If that wasn't enough to cause him trouble, Fields boasted that his on-screen and off-screen lives were inseparable. Few people disagreed with him. Even Carlotta Monti, his adoring and loyal mistress of many years, confessed, "They have said he was crochety, castigating, had a jaundiced eye, was larcenous, suspicious, shifty, erratic, frugal, and mercenary. I can only confirm these accusations." But her terrifying list doesn't do justice to his view of the world. He continuously expressed contempt for the bright and the slow, the strong and the weak, the rich and the poor, the old and the young, the sick and the healthy, as well as for children, mothers, relatives, racial groups, and *anyone else*. His hatred was awesome and total. To the day he died, Fields never changed. He never saw any reason to compromise with a universe he felt had maliciously decided to destroy him.

An advertisement for W. C. Fields' juggling routines
at the turn of the century.
Note the various props—e.g., cigar boxes, balls, hats—
all of which would become a famous part of his comedy act on the stage
and in the movies for forty-five years.

Given these facts, one wonders how this rogue got so many informed people to consider him the greatest comic of the twentieth century. Oliver Hardy, for example, thought Fields one of the most naturally funny men he had ever seen. Gene Buck, a highly respected talent scout in show business, called W. C. Fields one of the greatest comics that ever lived. Film commentators, drawn to the star's sense of defiance, saw in his style the most original approach to comedy ever put on film. Otis Ferguson, the noted film critic, summed up that position best: "If there ever was a great clown in the time of changeover from the beer and the music-hall to the universal distribution of radio and films, I would say it was in the person and the character and the undying if corny gusto of Bill Fields, who moved mountains until they fell on him, and then brushed himself off and looked around for more."

How is it possible, therefore, that this bigoted, pompous individual could not only make millions of people laugh but also get them to love him so much and for so long? Why, thirty years after his death, do so many scholars, historians, and critics acknowledge him as the noblest con man of them all?

No attempt to answer these questions can ignore Fields' childhood. For it was here that his hardships so dramatically shaped his future life and career. In this sense, he resembled Chaplin, who also had used his childhood tortures for film subjects and to inspire his screen "Charlie," the immortal tramp, a nostalgic, self-pitying, and romanticized clown who optimistically faced the world. Where W. C. Fields parted ways with Chaplin, however, was in Fields' using his childhood misery as film material for ridiculing rather than idealizing the people who had caused him pain. (It's no accident, therefore, that Fields hated Chaplin, and was clearly jealous over the success of Chaplin's artistry.)

If one were to accept Fields' version of his childhood, W.C. was a modern version of Oliver Twist: an outcast, a thief, a jailbird. Everyone he hated, so Fields would have us believe, was in one way or another a reminder of his youth.

Fields, born William Claude Dukenfield in Philadelphia, Pennsylvania, on January 29, 1880, was the oldest of five children (he had two brothers and two sisters). His father was James C. Duken-

W. C. Fields in his first movie, *Pool Sharks* (1915).
Evident are his early standard props:
his fake mustache and trick pool game.

field, a fruit and vegetable peddler of English descent, who only a few years before had emigrated to the United States. Not much is known about the background of Kate Felton, Fields' mother, except for his comments that she was native-born, lived next door to the recently arrived Dukenfields, and decided to marry because there was nothing else to do in Philadelphia after dark.

Growing up in the Dukenfield household must have been an ordeal. James, an unhappy husband and a demanding father as well as a poor businessman, considered his children nuisances and spent few happy moments with them. Kate had her hands full trying to care for the family's needs. She didn't have much time to spend with any one child. (Nevertheless, Fields and the other children remained devoted to her throughout their lives.) W.C. found his problems increasing with each passing year. Independent and aggressive by necessity, he grew to hate any form of regimentation. By the time he was nine years of age this hatred was directed against going to school and working for his father. The sensitive and stubborn boy actively searched for a way out of his detested routine. Supposedly the answer came to him one afternoon in 1889 while watching a juggling act at a local vaudeville theater. He decided then and there that he, too, would become a juggler. Fields, in later years, admitted that his choice was based on false information. He thought that since performers didn't report for work until the afternoon matinée, they had an easy life. What's more, he hated getting up early in the morning and felt this was the best way to avoid doing it. The truth is that Fields worked very hard at achieving his dream of becoming a juggler. He practiced sometimes as much as sixteen hours a day, anytime and anywhere he could, using anything and everything he could find. That discipline and drive paid off in the years to come, but the scars remained with him always. In a rare moment of honesty, Fields reflected in 1938 on what it was like for a ten-year-old boy who had his heart set on being famous: "I still carry scars on my legs from those early attempts at juggling. I'd balance a stick on my toes, toss it in the air, and try to catch it again on my toe. Hour after hour the damned thing would bang against my shinbones. I'd work until tears were streaming down my face. But I kept on practicing, and bleeding, until I perfected the trick. I don't believe that Mozart, Liszt, Paderewski, or Kreisler ever worked any harder than I did."

Bill's father didn't like the idea of his son's using the family vegetables for practice, and they fought often and bitterly. By the time he was eleven, W.C. found his relationship with his father unbearable and sought work elsewhere. It was about this time that he also quit school. At this point in the story Fields' version of the next eight years departs radically from the truth. While it's easy to dismiss his comment that he was thrown out of school for raping the teacher, it's harder to ignore his claim that he ran away from home and became an outcast in society, never sleeping in a bed, always sick, cold, and hungry. So often over the next sixty years did Fields tell that same Dickensian story that friends and foes

Fields as Eustace McGargle, with his ward (Carol Dempster),
in his first feature film, *Sally of the Sawdust* (1925).

alike believed it and used it as an explanation for the star's roguish
ways. But a recent book by his grandson claims that W.C. really
never left home until he was nineteen.

Closer to the truth, perhaps, is that after quitting his father's
employment, the daring youngster shifted for himself in the streets
of Philadelphia, which meant doing whatever was necessary to sur-
vive in a world where your parents don't have much time for you
and everyone else is indifferent as to whether you live or die. He
took whatever menial jobs he could, beginning with work in pool
halls and saloons, while at the same time gradually perfecting his
juggling. There is little doubt that he knew hunger, loneliness, and
fear; and even less doubt that he improved his status in the neigh-
borhood by becoming a first-class chisler, thief, and hustler. Street

Fields, with Alison Skipworth,
in *If I Had a Million* (1932).

life does not encourage honesty, and we can be certain that Fields did not remain honest very long.

But he paid a price for his independence. Constant fights with the other boys turned his nose into a monstrosity. (Fields always denied this, arguing instead that his bulbous nose resulted from heavy drinking at an early age.) His health also suffered from neglect and lack of proper medical care. At first respiratory problems transformed his voice into a nasal, rasping drawl, and then in later years came serious bouts with tuberculosis. And his constant insecurity over money, food, clothes, and shelter never really left him. In later years he originated one of the most unusual savings programs in history. Always fearful to the day he died that he would need money (despite his vast wealth), Fields made it a point to open savings accounts in banks wherever he went in America and abroad. Furthermore, to ensure that no one would know how much money he had, most accounts were opened under assumed names. He literally had money hidden around the globe . . . just in case! Some estimates say that at the time of his death Fields had over seven hundred bank accounts throughout the world.

Slowly but surely W.C.'s drive and ambition paid off. Between the ages of fourteen and nineteen his juggling improved to the point where he not only made money but also gained a respectable reputation as a first-rate juggler. Convinced of his talent, Fields finally left Philadelphia determined to become the best juggler in the world.

In fact, Fields became so confident that in 1900 he married Harriet Hughes and made her a part of his act. While they stayed together for a number of years, the marriage never really had a chance. "Even if he had married a girl who was a saint," explained the gifted writer Robert Lewis Taylor, "he would have been chafed by the double harness." The couple not only had religious differences (she was religious; he wasn't), but also he demanded complete freedom. Later on Fields would explain marriage by comparing a woman to an elephant. "They're nice to look at," he'd say, "but who wants to own one."

By the time he was twenty-one, there were few who did not know of his genius. The rising star and his wife were making trips across America and Europe, receiving rave reviews wherever they performed. The story is told how the great dramatic actress Sarah Bernhardt had a clause in her contract stating that she would never have to perform on the same program with a juggler, but she made an exception for Bill Fields.

It was in London, however, in 1901 that significant changes began to take place in the famous man's habits. Many of them had to do with his loneliness and insecurity, despite what appeared to be a happy marriage. For one thing, he felt uneducated and embarrassed by his lack of schooling, particularly among the English who prided themselves on their literacy. So one day, according to legend, Fields showed up with a trunk at a bookstore and told the owner to fill it with the best books around. Of all the great authors, none appealed

more to the sensitive star than Charles Dickens. For Fields, Dickens
had written only about him and about his Philadelphia youth. From
then on, almost every Fieldsian story somehow resembled a Dick-
·ens' tale. Many of Fields' biographers also point out that a popular
actor named Owen McGiveney was appearing with Fields that sea-
son and his specialty was impersonating a number of Dickens' characters. (It is not surprising that W.C.'s favorite characters were
Fagin, Scrooge, and Micawber.)

A second interest of Fields' at the turn of the century was
drawing. He decided to do cartoons to pass away the lonely hours
between shows and became quite good at it, eventually doing many
sketches for his own publicity posters.

Perhaps most significant was his new-found relief in drinking.
The strain and pressure of perfecting his juggling, the loneliness of
so many years, the growing distrust of his fellow man, his burning
desire to succeed all led him to liquor. By 1935 he was consuming
more than two quarts of alcohol a day. It got to the point where
his wardrobe consisted of three trunks, one for clothes and two for
liquor. When criticized for his drinking habits, he claimed they
were a preventative against snake bites, and he strongly recommended
that every actor carry with him one small snake. At the same time,
he explained that the best way to succeed was to disregard advice.
Fields arrived at that "simple" rule by observing the critical reactions that had greeted Wagner's operas, Lincoln's Gettysburg Ad-
dress, and Christ's Sermon on the Mount. So much for W.C.'s
opinion of critics.

But humor aside, by the early 1900s Fields' personal problems
were rapidly mounting. While he worked in the best theaters, began
to earn big money, and became a by-word in music halls everywhere, his marriage broke up after the birth of his son, his personality became more abrasive, and his health was set on a tragic path.
To Fields' credit, he never indulged in self-pity. Whatever criticisms
can be made about his life-style, and there were many, no one could
say that Bill Fields blamed anyone but himself for his mistakes.

In the years between 1900 and 1914, his fame increased. Triumph followed triumph, until he decided that he wanted more out
of life than the title "the world's greatest juggler" (which he had

given himself). So, in 1915, Fields went to work in the most glamorous showcase of the era, *The Ziegfeld Follies.*

Always trying to improve his act, Fields now began ad-libbing onstage. In the middle of a routine, for example, he'd pretend to lose his cigar and hat and then miraculously retrieve them without breaking his juggling pace. He also relied more heavily on the comedy skits in his repertoire, particularly those having to do with the frustration involved with playing golf and pool, as well as the evils of alcohol. Each of these skits would often reappear in Fields' movies over the next thirty years.

Another innovation in the period from 1914 to 1925, the Ziegfeld era, was the comedian's fascination with strange names. He kept a file of those names which amused him most and made it a practice of using them in his comedy routines and as pseudonyms for his screenwriting credits. Among his best were Chester Snavely, Egbert Sousé, Otis Criblecobis, Cuthbert J. Twillie, Figley J. Whitesides, Dr. Otis Guelpe, Larson E. Whipsnade, and Chester Bogle. The last one was his favorite, and he used it frequently. According to Fields, the real Bogle was a bootlegger whom Bill personally knew, but who never saw a Fields movie because Bogle's priest felt films were immoral.

In 1915, W. C. Fields made his film debut in *Pool Sharks,* a one-reel comedy short for the Gaumont Company. The simple plot had Fields competing with another fellow for a woman's love, but most of the screen time centered on the star's by now famous pool-game skit. (He had been using it onstage since 1903 and would later repeat the bit in a half-dozen movies up to 1944.) Working with a trick pool table he himself designed, Fields satirized the antics of the typical pool hustler who pretends incompetence and then with one final shot puts all fifteen balls into specific pockets on the table. The routine remains one of the classic comedy bits in screen and stage comedy. Fields is delightful as the aggressive, antisocial comic whose sense of timing and marvelous pantomime hold up remarkably well. Despite the fact that *Pool Sharks* and *His Lordship's Dilemma,* the second short that Fields made for the Gaumont Company, had no impact at the box office, the noted film historian William Everson expresses the opinion of many critics when he writes that *"Pool Sharks* must surely rank as one of the most auspicious debuts made by any of the major screen comedians." Nevertheless, Fields went back to the *Follies* and did not try his hand at movies for another ten years.

When he did return, the circumstances were somewhat changed. The chain of events which set that return in motion began in 1923. Fields, still trying to shed his "comic juggler" image, let it be known that he was interested in trying his luck in musical comedies. Hearing of Fields' "secret" ambitions, the producer of a new musical comedy, *Poppy*, offered the *Follies* star the part of Professor Eustace McGargle. The story had to do with McGargle, a small-time confidence man who travels the carnival world with Sally, a young girl who believes him to be her father. Actually the granddaughter of a wealthy family who had disowned her mother for marrying a circus man, Sally is eventually reunited with her family and their fortune while McGargle finds richer suckers to fleece. W.C. gladly accepted the part.

As you can imagine, the role of McGargle was ideal Fields material. (Whatever wasn't suited to Bill's taste at the start of rehearsals got rewritten by him before the Broadway opening of *Poppy* on September 3, 1923.) So perfectly did Fields enact the role of the lovable rascal with the top hat, baggy pants, and false mustache that when David Wark Griffith, the great silent film director, decided to make the popular play into a movie, there was no question that only Fields could play McGargle.

That was probably one of the few things that the two giants agreed on. Although they both enjoyed melodramas and loved Dickens, Griffith always emphasized the art of the film over the popularity of a star. The last person in the world, however, to feel that film style was more important than a screen personality was Bill Fields. Furthermore, W.C. had little respect for directors. As far as he was concerned, you either intimidated or ignored them. While acting in movies, he spoke only to those people he liked, and he liked few people, and never paid much attention to anything that didn't seem to be his idea. For that matter, Fields didn't think too highly of screenwriters either. As far as he was concerned, they could write whatever they wanted as long as they didn't show it to him.

In his first sound short for Mack Sennett, Fields played
an unsympathetic physician who is both a cheat and a sadist.
Here he is giving the sexy Elsie Cavanna the once over
in a scene from *The Dentist* (1932).

But unpleasant as W.C. was, he wasn't lazy or stupid. He just knew
what he could do best, and he felt his best was better than anything
else around.

Released in 1925, *Sally of the Sawdust* (the screen title of the
play) provided Fields with his first starring role, and he made the
most of it. Audiences enjoyed his portrayal of a pompous fraud who
violated traditional middle-class values while also throwing in some
first-rate juggling bits.

By now his years as a headliner in vaudeville and the *Follies*
had taught him how much everyday people enjoy laughing at the
idea that only the good succeed in society. Fields had almost per-

fected an image that was to make him one of the most unusual clowns in films. He reminded audiences that by never giving a "sucker" an even break, a chisler could do very well in the world.

Throughout his career Fields would argue that he was one of the few people in show business who really knew what was funny. One Fields law had to do with props. "It is never funny," as he once explained, "to break anything. It's only funny to bend things." In his early vaudeville days, for example, W.C. constantly broke cues during his pool routines. Few people laughed. Then he tried using a pewter cue which bent rather than broke and audiences roared. Another Fields law was that audiences love only an underdog. Make your clown rich and powerful, he argued, and you lose the public's love. Still another Fields law was to combine truth and surprise in your comedy routines. "Take this example," he stated. My daughter wants to throw a stone at a bad man. I stop her from throwing, shaking my head and giving her a little slap. My disapproval is complete. You think: 'That's right, she shouldn't throw a stone even at a villain.' Then I hand her a brick to throw. The bit of truth is that if you are going to strike, better hit hard."

But in 1925, Fields still needed to prove that his comedy was good box office. *Sally of the Sawdust,* while funny, had been only a modest commercial success. Nevertheless, Fields landed a contract with Paramount Pictures. Between 1926 and 1928 he made eight more feature films, mostly under the kindly supervision of William Le Baron, then production head of the company's Long Island Studio. Among the most popular of these ventures were *It's the Old Army Game* and *So's Your Old Man* (both made in 1926), *The Potters, Running Wild,* and *Two Flaming Youths* (all in 1927), and *Fools for Luck* (1928).

Even though these movies did poorly at the box office, they proved invaluable to Fields. Like Laurel and Hardy, Fields never changed his comic style or film material once he entered movies. He only perfected what he had done before. Making films at first was mostly an experiment to find out what did or did not work from his stage routines. Again like Laurel and Hardy, Fields used the successful material over and over in his silent and sound movies. Thus, for example, *So's Your Old Man* was remade in 1934 as *You're*

Fields and his "arch-rival," Baby LeRoy,
in a publicity shot on the set of *The Old Fashioned Way* (1934).

In 1935 Fields got to play his only straight acting film role.
The part was that of Mr. Micawber in MGM's production
of the Dickens classic *David Copperfield*.
Playing the part of the hero-worshipping David is Freddie Bartholomew.

Telling Me; parts of *It's the Old Army Game* appeared in *It's a Gift* (1934); and the best elements of *Two Flaming Youths* resurfaced in both *The Old Fashioned Way* (1934) and *You Can't Cheat an Honest Man* (1939). The fact that the later movies were in sound only furthered Fields' comedies. After all, much of his material gained its full impact from the unique voice and insulting manner that were so crucial to his comedy. Only a few silent clowns like Fields, Laurel, and Hardy really had the imagination to use sound effectively in the transitional years from 1927 to 1935. Even Chaplin needed many years to understand the importance of sound. Thus, as Everson points out in his wonderful book on Fields, looking at the star's sound films offers us a rare chance to see "that now-lost art of the vaudevillian's polishing of an act until it achieved perfection. . . ."

One of the most significant things that Fields did during those Long Island years was to develop a basic theory in which the routines of his antisocial clown could operate. According to Edward Sutherland, one of the two film directors who not only handled several of Fields' movies but also loved the star (the other director was Gregory La Cava), "Bill had only one story. It wasn't a story at all, really—there was just an ugly old man, an ugly old woman, and a brat of a child." Given these basic ingredients, he proceeded to attack every aspect of the so-called American way of life.

A good example of Fields' devastating attack on the American home takes place in *The Potters.* The story focuses on an average small-town family headed by Pa Potter (Fields) who "foolishly" robs his piggy bank and invests $4,000 in what appear to be worthless oil wells. After suffering abuse from his nagging wife for his "reckless" behavior, Potter becomes a hero when oil is actually discovered on the purchased land. In little more than an hour of screen time, Fields shows what it's like living with small minds and false values.

But Fields' movies were poorly made in the closing years of the twenties. In effect, Paramount's Long Island Studio was more interested in turning out movies than in producing first-rate films. Money, not art, was the studio's major concern, and the visual quality of its films left a lot to be desired. And, funny as W.C. was, he needed more freedom than he had to wisecrack and mutter his way through

42

the inhibiting plots. Of course, Paramount blamed Fields for the movies' bad box-office reception, and when his contract expired in 1928, they did not renew it.

Thus, at the moment that the "talkies" were taking charge, Fields found himself unacceptable to the movie industry. Although a big name in vaudeville and musical comedy, the forty-eight-year-old headliner seemed unable to establish a popular film image. It looked to most people as if his film days were over. Accepting a very generous offer to return to Broadway as the star of Earl Carroll's *Vanities of 1928* (a revue modeled after *The Ziegfeld Follies* and specializing in comedians and beautiful chorus girls), W.C. *apparently* had accepted the idea that movies were not for him. But it only seemed that way.

Over the next three years, Fields waited and watched the developments in sound films. Just to test the new system's possibilities, he made *The Golf Specialist* (1930), a twenty-minute short for RKO, and discovered that his potential for success in the movies was greater than ever before.

By 1931, Fields decided there was only one way to conquer the movies and that was to go to Hollywood, the film capital of the world, and devote his full time to screen comedy. By now there was no one who could stop him once he set himself on a course of action. With $350,000 in cash hidden throughout his clothes, and a new automobile, Fields left New York and the stage forever and drove across country to prove a point. He had no film contract, let alone a film offer.

Movie historians still shake their heads in awe over W.C.'s courage during the next eighteen months. He arrived dramatically on the Coast, pulling up to the most fashionable Hollywood hotel without any advance warning and demanding the bridal suite, explaining that, if necessary, he would comb the city for a bride to make his stay more acceptable to the hotel management. Not only didn't he get the room, but also no film company was willing to hire him. For more than a year, he tried to land a contract, willing even to work for nothing just to prove how good he was. But no one wanted him around.

Then Paramount finally agreed to take a gamble with what now seemed to be a humbled W. C. Fields. But the studio moved cautiously. Although he appeared in two movies in 1932 (*Million Dollar Legs* and *If I Had a Million*), Fields' screen time was kept to a minimum. In both films he appeared with many other stars, all of whom did "specialty" routines. In that way, Paramount had a chance to test which stars and comics the public liked best.

Despite all the limitations placed on him, Fields provided audiences with one of film history's classic routines in *If I Had a Million*. The movie itself featured such performers as Gary Cooper, George Raft, and Charles Laughton, all thrown together in separate episodes showing what happens to people when they are suddenly given a million dollars.

Fields' sequence dealt with a middle-aged couple (W.C. and the superb comedienne Alison Skipworth) who hate road hogs and spend their new-found money on a fleet of cars which are then used to attack inconsiderate motorists. This funny episode also provided a good look at the new Fields image. Gone was the fashionable, mustached bully of former years and in his place emerged a disreputable but lovable family man who was more sinned against than sinner. It was a comedy type that was to provide him with his greatest screen triumphs.

Fortunately for Fields, Mack Sennett during the early thirties was releasing his short films through Paramount. The studio agreed to let the two comedy geniuses work together for a brief period. If not for that, Paramount might have forced Fields to fit into their image of what they felt comedy ought to be. Reshaping one's image according to studio tastes was common practice in Hollywood during these years, and as many stars were destroyed as made by that process.

The Sennett-Fields collaboration prevented that from happening to Fields and resulted in four great comedy shorts: *The Dentist* (1932), *The Fatal Glass of Beer* (1932), *The Pharmacist*, and *The Barber Shop* (both in 1933). Throughout these hilarious two-reelers, the antisocial Fields offered some of the screen's most blistering pictures of small-town life. His absent-minded dentist cruelly and inconsiderately refers to his patients as "buzzards and palookas"; his barber, the local "maniac," straps customers into their chairs before burning them with hot towels; and his druggist spends most of his

Despite his declining health after 1935, Fields continued
to turn out funny movies. Here he is shown with his typical middle-class
screen family in a scene from *The Man on the Flying Trapeze* (1935).
From left to right: Grady Sutton, Vera Lewis, Mary Brian,
and Kathleen Howard (sitting on the bed).

time selling penny stamps and giving away free with each stamp sale
expensive vases. Throughout all these incredibly stupid acts, Fields'
character maintains his false dignity and sense of success.

Once more, however, Fields found himself in a confusing situation. On the one hand, the two-reeler format was perfect for his old
vaudeville routines, especially with the addition of sound. On the
other hand, Paramount decided to do with Fields what M-G-M had
done with Laurel and Hardy: the studio insisted that the comedian
now work only in feature films. In years to come, film critics and historians, as they did with Laurel and Hardy's move to features, would
argue that despite his one or two great feature films Fields should

Fields' success on the Edgar Bergen radio shows
gave the great clown a chance for a comeback at Universal Pictures.
Charlie McCarthy (the dummy) and Bergen, who had already
made a hit film for the studio, are shown here with Fields in his first
venture for his new studio, *You Can't Cheat an Honest Man* (1939).

have stayed with the two-reel format. What made matters even more confusing is that the more brilliant W.C. became in his short films, the more the public ignored him.

The classic situation appeared in connection with *The Fatal Glass of Beer* in 1932. Based upon his *Follies* material, the story told about Ma and Pa Snavely, a frontier couple whose only son, Chester (beautifully played by George Chandler), had gone to the city, fallen under the evil influence of alcohol, stolen some bonds, got sent to prison, and returned to his folks. Chester's greatest crime for his parents, however, was coming home without the bonds or any money. In the end, Ma and Pa throw Chester out into the cold, proving that without money there is very little love. This burlesque of Victorian sentimentality and morality did not sit well with Depression audiences in 1932. Desperate and hungry, they wanted to believe that they could depend on their loved ones in troubled times and didn't like being reminded that bad times bring few friends. But, as film historian Andrew Bergman so accurately said, "Fields saw decency and innocence as at best irrelevant, at worst positive obstacles." The great comedian, through his films, was saying, in effect, "Forget what you've been taught. This is a tough world where the only one you can depend upon is yourself. Learn that and act accordingly." Thus *The Fatal Glass of Beer* became one more example of where Fields' comedy was right and the world was wrong.

After finishing *The Barber Shop,* the Sennett-Fields collaboration ended, thereby saving a good personal friendship for both men. Paramount immediately put W.C. into another of their star-studded, loosely constructed movies, this one called *International House* (1933). Although Fields did not come on screen until the film was two-thirds over, his performance as a quack doctor proved so popular that the studio offered him a long-term contract. By now Fields had duly impressed the Paramount money men of his box-office strength, and he gave them a very tough time during the contract negotiations before he signed.

His first film under his new status was entitled *Tillie and Gus* (1933) and reunited him with Alison Skipworth. As usual, the plot was simple. Mistaken for missionaries, Gus (Fields) and Tillie (Skipworth) save a young couple and their baby from being swindled. Some of the film's best moments deal with Gus's jury trial in Alaska and the attempt to hustle Gus (disguised as a missionary) in a poker game. What most audiences remember best is Fields' oft-quoted remark in answer to the question "Do you like children?" "I do," he says, "if they're properly cooked."

The film also brought Fields his first contract with the child actor Baby LeRoy, the source of many legendary anecdotes about the star's intense dislike for the screen-stealing infant. The most famous story, however, occurred in their third film together, *It's a Gift* (1934). Determined to punish Baby LeRoy for his "intentional" upstaging of Fields, the paranoid fifty-four-year-old clown offered to care for

LeRoy while his nurse went to the powder room. As soon as the unsuspecting lady left, Fields filled the baby's bottle full of gin, making it impossible in a few minutes for the child to stand, let alone walk. As the frantic crew tried to revive Baby LeRoy, Fields kept shouting, "Walk him around! Send him home! The kid's no trouper!" Fields' fans, in an effort to save their hero's reputation, claimed the star felt guilty over his treatment of Baby LeRoy and often brought the child toys to play with. Fields' enemies point out that some of the toys included bowie knives and hatchets.

In any case, between 1933 and 1938, the great clown appeared in eleven Paramount feature films, including *The Old Fashioned Way* (1934), *The Man on the Flying Trapeze* (1935), and *Poppy* (1936). Furthermore, Fields finally got to play the role of Micawber in 1935, when the studio agreed to let him appear in M-G-M's *David Copperfield*.

In the judgment of most critics, the best film of his entire Paramount career was *It's a Gift*, a merciless attack on small-town life. Fields played the role of Harold Bissonette, the inept owner of a general store whose life and values are forever in conflict with his relatives and customers. Determined to escape from his troubles, Bissonette buys an orange ranch through the mail and moves his family West. Of course, the orange grove is a disaster area, but by a stroke of luck he sells the land to race-track promoters and takes the cash to buy a good orange grove.

Only once more in his career (in 1940) would Fields ever reach such comic heights as he did in *It's a Gift*. His mannerisms and absurd behavior as the stoical husband frustrated by family, society, and inanimate objects are a masterpiece of comic creation. Only Fields, struggling against what appears unbeatable odds, could produce such laughter. Since he wrote the script (by now standard practice in any Fields film), the cynical portraits of small-town family life were screen gems. To cite just one example out of many, Bissonette is having breakfast with his horrible family. For a few moments he watches his eight-year-old son monopolize the sugar and then whacks the boy. "What's the matter, Pop?" the brat asks. "Don't you love me anymore?" Before Bissonette can hit the boy again, his shrewish wife shrieks, "Don't you touch that child." Incensed, Bissonette answers, "He's not going to tell me I don't love him." Such scenes and dialogue plus Fields' mutterings about life and people combine to make the film an absolute delight.

Unfortunately for the neurotic clown, he was never meant to enjoy fame and happiness at the same time. By the mid-1930s, his distrust of doctors and his refusal to modify his drinking habits combined to break his health permanently. For months, the proud star allowed people to think him drunk rather than tell them the truth (in fact, Fields rarely appeared drunk and refused to be friends with anyone who did except those who were already his friends). In the years from 1935 on, he suffered from various illnesses as well as the horrors of alcoholism, including nightmares and hallucinations.

From 1936 to 1939 he spent some of the most miserable days and nights anyone could imagine. Unable to sleep, frightened of imaginary robbers, kidnappers, and bandits, Fields still refused to follow medical advice. His usual joke was that when doctors and undertakers meet, they wink at each other. Finally, he withdrew to a sanitarium to recover his strength.

But those who thought W.C. was through were wrong. Although he still didn't have the strength to make movies, he had his wit and his voice, and in 1937 radio wanted him. So he took to the airwaves as a regular guest on Edgar Bergen and Charlie McCarthy's "Chase and Sanborn Hour." Once more, Fields became a household word as he exchanged verbal gags with the dummy McCarthy. In 1939 he got his own show for Lucky Strike cigarettes, and one of his constant gags became talking about his "son," Chester Field.

By 1938 the master showman felt strong enough to return to Paramount. The studio, however, was not overjoyed to have him back. In their eyes, the days of the great clowns were over. This was the era of comedy films based on witty scripts and using imaginative directors. Sound movies, so the studio felt, needed more than just a strong personality. To prove their point, Paramount put him in another of their star-studded productions, *The Big Broadcast of 1938* (a movie which also introduced to film audiences a new clown by the name of Bob Hope singing "Thanks for the Memories"). The movie was not a success although Fields received good reviews for his dual performance as a millionaire playboy and his tightwad broth-

Fields in his classic role as Egbert Sousé in *The Bank Dick* (1940).
Grady Sutton plays the slow-witted Og Oggilby.

er. More convinced than ever that the fifty-nine-year-old comic was
through, Paramount refused to renew his contract.

Fortunately for film history, Universal Pictures decided to hire
Fields. The situation at that studio was somewhat similar to Roach's
situation back in the mid-twenties when he experimented with his
All-Star films. In the closing years of the thirties Universal decided
to reorganize the studio's film production around the idea of low-
budget family entertainment instead of trying to compete with big
studios like Paramount and M-G-M. The trouble was that they didn't
have any big names to attract audiences. So mainly for that reason,
Universal figured it might get some box-office power by just having
Fields appear in their movies.

That may have been their opinion of the star's ability, but Fields

Considered by some as a minor masterpiece,
Never Give a Sucker an Even Break (1941) was Fields' last starring role.
Here he is shown in his famous restaurant exchange with Jody Gilbert.

certainly didn't share it. He made that very clear in their contract talks, in which he demanded—and got—$150,000 for each film, $25,000 of which was for his scriptwriting chores. (Scriptwriting, for Fields, meant jotting some notes down on scraps of paper which he later discarded during shooting if he felt the urge to do so.)

Universal could not have made a better deal. At almost sixty years of age, Fields proved to be more brilliant than ever in his comedy roles. The four starring films that he made for the studio between 1939 and 1941 remain classic models of his unique comic genius.

First came *You Can't Cheat an Honest Man* (1939), in which Fields capitalized on his famous radio fight with Charlie McCarthy and Edgar Bergen. As Larson E. Whipsnade, the shifty but lovable circus owner who is determined to see his daughter happily married, Fields has one delightful battle after another with his employees, McCarthy and Bergen. Among the best verbal gags are his labeling of McCarthy as "a flophouse for termites" and "a woodpecker's snack bar." Not to be outdone, Charlie delivers the unforgettable retort, "Why you two-legged martini, you weren't born, you were squeezed out of a bar rag."

The second Universal movie was *My Little Chickadee* (1940), which for the first and only time teamed Fields with the one person in the world who could match him in antisocial comedy, the incredible Mae West. (To understand the significance of that unusual event, it's best to discuss the movie in the next chapter, which is devoted to this very special woman.)

Then in the latter half of 1940 came the greatest of all Fields' movies, *The Bank Dick*. Written, according to legend, by the star on toilet paper while he was in the bathroom and submitted under the pseudonym of Mahatma Kane Jeeves, the story summarized his view of middle-class life in a small town.

Fields played the part of Egbert Sousé, a hapless husband dwelling in the town of Lompoc and saddled with a nagging wife who insisted that her obnoxious mother live with the family, which also includes two creepy daughters, the oldest of whom is determined to marry the town fool. What there was of a traditional plot had to do with Fields first convincing his future son-in-law (well played by Grady Sutton) to embezzle bank funds to buy worthless stock in a gold mine and then trying to protect the sucker when the bank examiner (brilliantly enacted by Franklin Pangborn) arrives earlier than expected.

The gags and comic situations move so quickly that it's almost impossible to find one scene that is funnier than another. Everything that society considers sacred in family relationships and work habits is debunked by Fields and his cast over and over again, so that by the film's conclusion we are left amazed at the skill in which the plot and subplots have been masterfully orchestrated.

Fields' final triumph came in 1941 with the release of *Never Give a Sucker an Even Break*. The illogical plot had Fields playing himself and trying to sell Esoteric Studios a film story that could never be made. It was to be his swan song on the stupidities of film production. But the movie's most memorable scene involves the great man eating lunch in a greasy restaurant run by a heavy, sarcastic waitress (superbly played by Jody Gilbert). One of the more classic exchanges between the two takes place as Fields complains about his meals. "And another thing," says the waitress, "you're always squawking about something. If it ain't the steak, it's something else." Fields mutters back, "I didn't squawk about the steak, dear. I merely said I didn't see that old horse that used to be tethered outside here."

Despite the irrelevant plot, *Never Give a Sucker an Even Break*, like the other Universal films, proved successful at the box office, and it would have been marvelous if Fields could have kept up his pace. But, once again, his health gave out. Try as he did in the next few years to work himself into even a minor part, the amazing man finally found it impossible to bounce back.

In the mid-1940s, Fields once more withdrew to a sanitarium and waged his last fight with "the fellow in the bright nightgown" (his name for death). Ironically, the end came on Christmas Day, 1946, as if to prove that a hostile universe wanted him to die on the most sentimental day in the year and the one which he hated most. Perhaps it's just as well that he died as he did. He always refused to knuckle under to this hostile world, and legend has it that just seconds before "the fellow in the bright nightgown" took him from us, Bill Fields opened his eyes and winked. He was no fool.

THE FUNNIEST BAD GIRL

MAE WEST

Women have never felt kindly toward the great clowns like Stan Laurel, Oliver Hardy, and W. C. Fields. Not only don't these men project any sex appeal, but they also go out of their way to present their screen women as enemies or mindless sex objects. If there is one great clown, however, who has won the hearts of both men and women, it is Mae West, the wisecracking, brazen actress with the hourglass figure. The screen image she offers her fans flatters a woman's ego while, at the same time, tickling a male's fancy. Based upon the character of Diamond Lil, the Bowery songstress she created on the New York stage in 1928, Miss West in all of her movies ridicules the popular vamp and dumb blonde stereotypes: glamorous, witty, tough, and big-hearted, the free-swinging lady takes charge of her own affairs. Every male is viewed in terms of what he can do for her and not the other way around. No matter what she says, her slow, nasal drawl makes the dialogue sound spicy. And no one gives this woman any trouble. What she wants, she gets, because she is clever and better than the men whom she often calls "suckers!" But, like all of the memorable clowns in screen history, her greatest asset in comedy is her appeal to our imagination. She makes us realize how funny sex really is.

Her outspokenness, however, made Mae West one of the most controversial film stars of the thirties. Mary Pickford, for example, found her "shocking." Reviewers called her works "crude" and "vulgar." And censors worked feverishly to prevent her movies from even being made. But she had on her side the most powerful ally a talented performer could ever have: the public. Adolph Zukor, the founder of Paramount Pictures and a man who ought to know the facts, wrote, "When you speak of an era, Mae was in command during the depression years." *Playboy* concurred, stating, "Along with Garbo and Shirley Temple, she was the hottest box-office draw in the land and probably the best-known, most photographed person on earth." Steven V. Roberts, the Los Angeles bureau chief of *The New York Times*, summed it all up by declaring, "There is no other Mae West. She is an institution, a living legend, as much a part of the American folklore as Paul Bunyan or Tom Sawyer or Babe Ruth."

At the heart of the controversy over the Westian character, as well as over those images created by such roughhouse comedians as Fields, Don Rickles, and Mel Brooks, is the issue of taste. No one denies that people differ in their tastes, or that it's foolish to argue simple matters of personal preference. The issue is whether or not there are absolute standards that cultured and educated people can use to judge whether something is in "good" or "bad" taste. Those who argue in favor of these absolute standards are not opposed so much to violence and sex as they are to the manner in which these subjects are treated. In particular, those who attacked West's comedy did so because of the manner in which she treated sex. A typical example of the Westian approach which might illustrate the critics' objections is her comment, "Good women are no fun. . . . The only good woman I can recall in history was Betsy Ross. All she ever made was a flag." Or her famous wisecrack, "It's not the men in my life that counts—it's the life in my men." To those who argue for good taste, Mae West's dialogue and mannerisms are "nasty," "infantile," and "vicious." But to Mae West and the millions who love her, Westian comedy is a great way to kid the pants off of society's sexual hypocrisy. No one has ever done a better job or worked harder at destroying through comedy the outmoded sexual double standards for men and women than Mae West. And she started long before she came to Hollywood.

Mae West was born in Brooklyn, New York, on August 17, 1893. She was the first of three children born to Patrick and Matilda West. Her father was a livery stable owner of English-Irish descent. Known as "Battling Jack," the lightweight boxing champion of Brooklyn at at the time of his marriage, he later became first a private detective when cars replaced horse-drawn carriages and then ended his days selling real estate. It was from him that Mae derived her toughness, intense dislike of tobacco, and a soft spot for boxers. Throughout her career she made it a practice to give work to ex-boxers by finding parts for them in her plays and films. From her mother, who had been born in Germany, emigrated to America in 1882, and found work as a corset and fashion model, Mae derived her views on health and life. Although a stern woman with the younger children, Beverly and John, Mrs. West clearly favored Mae and indulged the older girl's moody behavior, convinced that she was someone very special.

By the time she was seven, Mae's interest in the theater led her to "Professor" Watts Dancing School on Fulton Street in Brooklyn. Within two weeks West had convinced her teacher she should compete in amateur contests, and to everyone's surprise but hers, she began winning one contest after another. It took some convincing to get her indulgent parents to let her enter as many amateur nights as she did, but Mae was determined to work on the stage. Before a year had passed, "Baby Mae," as she billed herself, grew tired of her amateur standing and gladly accepted, with her parents' permission, Hal Clarendon's offer to join his Brooklyn stock company. From 1901 to 1904, the independent youngster played such well-known children's parts as Little Nell, Little Eva, and Little Lord Fauntleroy. For those stage productions in which no children's parts were needed, Mae entertained the Brooklyn crowds during the play's intermissions, doing delightful song-and-dance imitations of famous headliners like Eddie Foy and George M. Cohan. When not actually performing, she studied theater life, especially the tricks of the profession in reaching and capturing the favor of an audience. It was during this period as well that Mae developed her famous speaking style of slowly pronouncing the syllables of long words. According to Mae, the practice started as a result of her love for vocabulary and the pleasure she got from rhythmically sounding out words like "fas-cin-a-tion."

Understandably, her school work suffered and not even private tutors could salvage her fragmented public school training. So, at thirteen, everyone connected with Mae agreed that her formal education should end. No doubt West's teachers marveled in later years at her success, particularly in arithmetic where the Westian definition of addition was "Two and two makes four, and five will get you ten if you know how to work it."

The well-developed youngster by now had discovered not only that she was quite popular with boys but also that she adored their attention and the games they played together. From the moment she made that discovery Mae West made it a point never to be without a handful of admirers. It was for this reason, Mae immodestly explained, that she was always able to write parts in her plays and films for half a dozen men. As she said, "I had that in real life."

Mae West in her riotous stage play
Diamond Lil (1928).

The three years with Clarendon had taught Mae that she preferred the spotlight to supporting roles. As a result, the ambitious
fourteen-year-old singer entered the tough, competitive vaudeville
world where child acts were popular favorites with audiences, the
best acts of the day featuring teen-agers like Buster Keaton and Fred
Astaire. Over the next few years she worked hard at her trade, singing and dancing as well as writing a number of her own songs.
Before very long she met and teamed up with Frank Wallace, a
song-and-dance man who was the only male in her life to get Mae
West to the altar. The couple were married on April 11, 1911,
but they were clearly mismatched and within a few months both
the marriage and the act broke up. Unfortunately for Mae, she

didn't divorce Frank until 1943 (mainly because of laziness) and it cost her considerable discomfort during the thirties. (Although she has gone with many men in her life, she has never married again, and Mae makes it a practice never knowingly to date a man who is married.)

Having separated from her husband, West felt she was ready for the big time, New York vaudeville. By persevering she soon got a chance to show her talents one Sunday night at the Columbia Theater in Manhattan, the one evening in the week when the busy booking agents and producers assembled to screen the new acts in town. Producer Ned Wayburn took an interest in the eighteen-year-old performer and signed her to a part in his new revue.

Wayburn's show was entitled A La Broadway and Hello, Paris, a revue that opened at the Fulton Theater on September 22, 1911. Two men connected with the revue and Mae's Broadway debut were the writer William Le Baron (who later went on to Paramount Pictures to produce not only many of her films but also those of Fields) and the producer Jesse Lasky (who shortly thereafter brought Cecil B. DeMille to the movies and helped build Paramount Studios). So effective were Mae's renditions of dialect and ragtime songs that she attracted the attention of the famous Broadway producers the Schuberts, who two months later put her in their new musical production Vera Violetta, starring a blackfaced Al Jolson. (Interestingly, this was the revue in which the twenty-five-year-old Jolson began his routine of leaving the stage during the show and singing and dancing in the aisles.) Good as she was, West appeared in only one more musical, A Winsome Widow, playing the amusing role of La Petite Daffy, and then she returned to vaudeville.

The Mae West that vaudeville audiences now saw was a lot different from the inexperienced youngster who had gone to Broadway seeking fame and fortune. For one thing she had become a big name and was able to command salaries of from $350 to $750 a week, depending upon the time and the place. Secondly, she began introducing suggestive sexual overtones into her dancing and singing. In her humorous and candid autobiography, Goodness Had Nothing to Do With It, Mae claims that she wasn't fully aware of the changes in her that were taking place on the stage. "It wasn't what I did,"

When George Raft suggested West for the role of
his fast-talking girl friend in his new film *Night After Night* (1932),
he had no idea she would steal the picture from him.
Here the two stars pose for a publicity shot for the movie.

she wrote, "but how I did it. It wasn't what I said, but how I said it; and how it looked when I did and said it. I had evolved into a sex symbol and didn't know it." But during the years from 1912 to 1918, the famous Westian mannerisms took shape: the suggestive walk, the sultry movement of her hands to her hair and hips, and the teasing use of double entendres, such as "I like a man who's good, but not too good—for the good die young, and I hate a dead one."

It was also during this period that she met and developed a life-long friendship with the New York attorney James A. Timony, who after surviving his romantic interest in Mae became her manager and adviser until his death in 1954.

Her first chance to appear in movies came in 1918, when she had returned to Broadway to appear in Rudolf Friml's *Showtime* (where many people credit her with introducing the dance sensation of the day, the "shimmy"). One night after the show, Jack Dempsey, the then reigning heavyweight champion of the world, came backstage and discussed the possibility of her working with him in a proposed film serial entitled *Daredevil Jack*. The idea appealed to her and the two made a short screen test for Pathe films, but the project never went any further. Instead, Mae accepted a big contract to go back into national vaudeville.

Good as she was, she still worked the second-class circuits. Now in her mid-twenties, Mae found doing three performances a day too demanding. What she wanted was a major showcase on Broadway and her own starring role. But nothing she was offered suited her tastes. Finally her mother suggested that Mae do what she had been doing for years in vaudeville, write her own material. It took a lot of nerve to write and produce her own play, but as West often said over the years, there's nothing like success to excuse one's actions. The show was entitled *Sex*, and it opened in New York at Daly's Theater on April 26, 1926. The Westian character was named Margie LaMont, a Montreal prostitute who wiggled out of one tight spot after another. Not only wouldn't the newspapers accept ads for the play, but the reviewers tore into the star and the show, calling it "a dirty play," "low entertainment," and "crude . . . inept." *The Herald Tribune* labeled its review "*Sex* Wins High Mark for Depravity, Dullness." But, from its opening night until the following year, the public flocked to see the brazen actress perform. The play might have gone on for another year, except for the emergence in early 1927 of a reform group calling itself the Society for the Suppression of Vice. Powerful enough to influence the city officials, these moral crusaders got the police to crack down on three Broadway shows, one of which was *Sex*. Following raids on February 21, 1927, West, her manager, and her producer were arrested, charged with writing an obscene show and giving lewd performances on stage. Two months later, the West group was convicted, fined $500 each, and both Mae and Timony were sentenced to ten days in jail for "corrupting the morals of youth." The trial made Mae West a national sensation and she milked the publicity for all it was worth, making even more news when she won the right to wear her own silken panties because prison underwear was too rough on her skin. She served only eight days, claiming that this was the only time in her career that she ever got anything for good behavior.

Encouraged by her success with *Sex*, Mae wrote a second play, *The Drag*, dealing with the tragic life of a homosexual and the problems his unconventional desires cause his loved ones. To this day the problems of homosexuals remain a serious interest to West. "I've liked 'em since vaudeville," she explained in 1971, "when I used to take some of the chorus boys home. My mother, whom I was crazy about, loved 'em 'cause they'd fix her hair and her hats. They were all humorous, sweet, talented and some, geniuses." Although she didn't appear in *The Drag* (she was starring in *Sex* at the time) Mae produced and opened the show in Paterson, New Jersey, in 1926. It attracted widespread attention, too much, in fact, to satisfy the New York crusaders who successfully persuaded Mae not to bring it to Broadway. By now convinced that she alone knew how to write her kind of shows, Mae devoted full time to creating her own material. Nothing she ever did, however, was as successful as her story of a well-kept Bowery saloon singer living during the 1890s: *Diamond Lil*. Filled with nostalgia and free-wheeling comedy, the show had, its premiere performance at Teller's Schubert Theater in Brooklyn on April 9, 1928. The part of Lil established once and for all the Westian character: an earthy, bawdy woman who dominates the

West as Lady Lou setting her traps for love-stricken
Captain Cummins (Cary Grant) in *She Done Him Wrong* (1933).

world in which she lives, makes majestic entrances wearing tight-
fitting jeweled gowns and trailing a train which she often kicks
dramatically aside; on her head she sports a wide-brimmed hat with
the crown cut away so that her blond hair looks regal. But best of
all is the manner in which she puts down male society. A good
illustration is the exchange between Mae and an admirer. "Your
hands," the poor fellow gasps, "your lips, your hair, your magnifi-
cent shoulders. . . ." Smirking, Mae interrupts, "What're you doin',
honey? Makin' love or takin' inventory?" From that show on, it
became difficult to tell where the public and private Mae West dif-
fered. She herself has said often, "I'm her and she's me and we're
each other. Lil and I, in my various characterizations, climbed the
ladder of success, wrong by wrong."

Stimulated by the phenomenal success of *Diamond Lil* and continuing her fascination with female impersonators, Mae wrote and opened a second play on Broadway entitled *Pleasure Man*, a backstage romantic melodrama. Within two days of its opening, the police raided the show and West was once more back in the headlines. This time, however, she won the case but lost interest in reopening the play.

The years from 1929 to 1932 followed the by now familiar Westian pattern of reviving past successes, going on national tours, and creating new material for Broadway. Fortunately for movie history, the Depression hit stage performers very hard, and as 1932 rolled around many New York actors were out of work and heading toward California, where the movies, because of the new sound invention, paid big money for Broadway talent with good, unusual voices.

One such performer who had gone to Hollywood and knocked around for a while was George Raft, the tough kid from Hell's Kitchen in New York who, in his long career, has been an internationally famous dancer, prize fighter, sportsman, friend of the underworld, and a memorable screen tough guy. By 1932, Raft was ready for his first starring role for Paramount Pictures in *Night After Night*. The story was tailor-made for him. He played the part of Joe Anton, an ex-boxer and prohibition tough guy who runs a New York speakeasy and gambling casino but wants to make it big in high society. Determined to please Raft, the studio (intent on turning him into a new Valentino) gave him the right to choose the other members of the cast. For the role of Anton's former girl friend, Maudie, he selected Mae West. Raft and West had met casually over the years mainly because Raft's mobster friend Owney Madden had secretly financed one of West's shows in the mid-twenties. This provided Madden with a cover for his protection racket, thus enabling gangsters to drop off their collections backstage at the theater on Saturday nights. It was Raft's job because of his show business work and familiarity with performers to pick up the money for Madden. So George saw and knew West's style very well.

Getting Mae to come to Hollywood in the summer of 1932 was not difficult. Paramount gave her a $5,000 a week contract, and for someone well aware of the financially bad Broadway scene, the deal seemed perfect. But if Hollywood thought they were getting some starry-eyed stage comedian eager, like Fields, to prove herself in movies, they were in for a shock. Mae let them know right from the start who she was. "I'm not a little girl from a small town makin' good in a big town," stated the Broadway bad girl. "I'm a big girl from a big town makin' good in a small town."

After waiting around for a few weeks with nothing to do but pick up her weekly checks, Mae reconsidered her small part in the film and decided to call it quits. She wanted out of her contract and was heading home. Fortunately for Paramount, the film's producer was Le Baron, who was brilliant at handling the likes of West and Fields. He told Mae to rewrite her part according to her own taste and then made sure that her scenes were shot and edited to West's best advantage. This made a lot of old-timers in Hollywood shake their heads in wonder. After all, Mae West was an aging sex symbol fast approaching forty years of age who had never once proved her drawing power at movie box offices. Then came Mae's first entrance on the screen in what may well be the single greatest opening bit in any film actress's career. The scene was Anton's nightclub and in walks his former girl friend, well dressed and covered with jewels. The wide-eyed hat-check girl, overwhelmed by the lady, remarks, "Goodness, what beautiful jewelry." As if unaware of the remark, Maudie walks toward the long flight of stairs leading up to the gambling rooms, then stops, turns slowly around, and purrs, "Goodness had nothing to do with it, dearie." She then swaggers up the stairs. In short, West was a sensation. Raft summed up just how good his choice had been saying, "It was her first screen appearance and her cleverness onstage was a new kind of thievery to me. She stole everything but the cameras and I never made another picture with her."

Sensing they had a gold mine in Mae West, the Paramount executives pleaded with her to do another picture for them, this time in a starring role. She agreed, mainly on the condition that the film would be a screen version of *Diamond Lil*. But as much as the studio wanted her, the idea caused a problem. The studio's story department insisted that the typical movie audience, supposedly made up

West and a grateful Adolf Zukor, whose Paramount Studios
were saved by the star's successful films,
posing for a picture on the set of *I'm No Angel* (1933).

of young people from eight to twenty-two years of age, would never go for a costume picture about the Gay Nineties. Mae disagreed, and she convinced the studio to let her try. Part of the reason she was able to get her way was because West insisted that she could make the film in three weeks instead of the usual four months that Paramount took to produce its big budget movies.

The final delay in shooting *She Done Him Wrong*, the film's title, was in finding a leading man. Everyone tested for the part failed to satisfy Mae. And then, one day, according to her recollection, she caught a glimpse of Cary Grant walking across the studio lot. He looked so "sensational" that all Mae wanted to know was if he could talk. Nearer to the truth perhaps, is that Grant had already proven that he was an actor on the rise. He had just finished a strong performance opposite Paramount's reigning sex queen, Marlene Dietrich, in *Blonde Venus*, and Lowell Sherman, the film's director, had already been signed to direct the new West movie.

Shooting on *She Done Him Wrong* began in late November 1932 and within eighteen days one of the most memorable films in screen comedy had been completed. It opens with a series of short sketches that set the mood of the Gay Nineties and the atmosphere in Gus Jordan's saloon, and we see the kind of people that make up Lady Lou's world. Before meeting Lou (Mae West) we learn that she is the mistress of Gus (played by Noah Beery, Sr.), a man who not only runs a Bowery beer hall but also, unknown to Lou, traffics in white slavery and counterfeit money. Then into the movie comes Lady Lou, with typical Westian style and wit. Descending from her carriage, she affectionately pats a child's head and his mother lovingly remarks what a fine woman Lou is. Lou purrs back, "One of the finest women who ever walked the streets." From that remark on, the movie's pace and vitality never flag as the usual large assortment of cast and quips unfolds. Drawn romantically to a detective secretly disguised as Captain Cummings of the Salvation Army (Cary Grant), Lou unwittingly helps to destroy Gus's criminal activities and to send him to jail.

The most memorable aspects of *She Done Him Wrong*, in addition to her highly suggestive singing of songs like "I Wonder Where My Easy Rider's Gone" and "A Guy What Takes His Time," are the gags between West and her superb supporting cast. There is the exchange, for example, between the deflowered Little Sally (Rochelle Hudson), a victim of white slavery, and the understanding Lou. Sally is convinced that no one will ever want her after what she's done, but Lou wisely explains, "When women go wrong, men go right after 'em." Another famous exchange takes place when Cummings and Lou meet for the first time and she teases him by saying, "Why don't you come up some time, 'n see me?" and "Come up, I'll tell your fortune." When he resists her charms, she senses his real desires and mutters, "Aw, you can be had." In the end, she gets everything her way. Sitting alone with Cummings, whom she knows to be a policeman, she lets him put a diamond ring on her finger. "You bad girl," he slyly says, and Lou replies, "You'll find out."

She Done Him Wrong turned out to be a box-office sensation, proving for the moment that Mae knew better than anyone else what Depression audiences wanted. Those who looked on her as a vulgar woman parading her charms tastelessly for money never really understood her genius. Uneducated as she was, she understood life and the hypocrisy that surrounds our everyday existence. "Throughout all the comic exchanges and verbal gags," John Tuska wisely wrote, "a philosophy of life is woven, a world-view which invites us to take life as it is, not to change it, nor pretend that it doesn't exist, but to accept it and, wherever possible, take advantage of it." In short, she saw the human condition as it was and said so.

She Done Him Wrong contains several racial slurs that did not bother white audiences in the thirties. Like Fields and other ex-vaudevillians, West worked ethnic jokes into her shows and films. Throughout her career in show business such material proved popular with American audiences everywhere. (In fact, ethnic humor, although treated somewhat differently, is currently enjoying a renaissance on television with hit shows like "All in the Family," "Sanford and Son," "Chico and the Man," and "Happy Times.") But the movies in the thirties forced most black performers to play almost all their parts as dumb, lazy, and farcical servants. White audiences and clowns rationalized the practice by saying that it was all in good fun. It wasn't, and anyone who takes the time to read the black press of the period can easily find out why. The point here is not to defend

Another publicity shot on the set of *I'm No Angel*,
this time highlighting Cary Grant and producer William Le Baron.
The obviously stagestruck script girl is unknown.

Mae West, but to explain that racial humor was the practice and that she went along with the tide. Illustrative of how such comedy worked is the exchange between Lady Lou and her maid Pearl (played by the very talented Louise Beavers, who, in 1934, won international fame for her role in *Imitation of Life*). Hearing Lou yelling for her, Pearl replies in plantation dialect, "I'se comin', I'se comin'." And Lou responds, "You're comin', you're comin', your head is bendin' low. Get here before winter." In several of the West films such racial humor occurs, with the parts of black maids being played by such gifted actresses as Gertrude Howard, Libby Taylor, and Hattie McDaniel. The reader no doubt remembers that Hattie McDaniel became the only black actress to win an Academy Award for her 1939 performance of Mammy in *Gone With the Wind*.

In 1933, however, the last thing on Paramount's mind was racial slurs. For a number of years the studio had been struggling to stay alive, existing from one picture to the next in a desperate attempt to find the right film formula for Depression audiences. Mae West was it. According to Le Baron, *She Done Him Wrong* must be credited with having saved Paramount studios at a time when the studio was considering selling out to M-G-M and when Paramount theaters—seventeen hundred of them—thought of closing their doors and converting their theaters into office buildings. Sensing her great popularity, the studio publicized her name around the globe. Within months, West was influencing contemporary fashions and providing answers on how to attract lovers and on how to keep a man happy. Arthur Mayer, in his delightful book *Merely Colossal*, recalls the time when as Paramount's publicity director he ran into difficulty with studio head Zukor over the term "lusty" as a label for Mae West. Mayer kept insisting that the term meant "vigorous" and "full of life," but Zukor screamed, "No one needs to tell me what 'lusty' means. When I look at her chest, I know what lusty means."

Zukor wasn't the only one upset with the West publicity. Once again, the free-wheeling lady had caught the attention of a reform group, only this time her opponents were the motion picture censors. Because what took place in 1933–34 was so important for the next twenty years in Hollywood movie-making, we need to consider briefly what Mae West was up against.

Ever since movies began in the mid-1890s, church and reform groups had insisted that the film industry exerted a negative influence on American life. The first serious threat that these reformers presented to Hollywood came in the early 1920s when a number of scandals involving major film personalities shocked the nation. Forced to defend themselves from federal, state, and local censorship legislation, the film industry hired William H. Hays, the then Postmaster General of the United States, under the pretext of "cleaning up the movies." For a while, it looked as if William Hays could do the job, and criticism against Hollywood subsided. But then came the Depression and the falling box-office receipts. Eager to win back audiences, the money-minded movie executives ignored Hays's warnings and began flooding the screens with sensational stories about gangsters, gun molls, and decent women forced into prostitution. Once more the censors rose up in anger, this time claiming that the new treatment of sex and violence would condition the public to think that crime and prostitution were acceptable ways of life. Determined to prevent that from happening, religious groups in general and the Roman Catholic Church in particular descended on the Hays Office. Hays, in turn, predicted that unless the film producers changed their ways, the film industry was doomed. The studio executives took Hays seriously, encouraging him to draft a code that might satisfy the religious crusaders. Working with Martin Quigley and Reverend Daniel A. Lord, the former a powerful Catholic layman and the latter a Jesuit priest, Hays produced the highly controversial document "A Code to Govern the Making of Motion and Talking Pictures." Almost three-quarters of the code dealt with the treatment of screen sex. The plan was to have someone from Hays's office approve film scripts before films could be produced. But the producers shrewdly insisted on paying the salary of the man who did the supervising. We have only to remember West's dialogue in *Night After Night* and *She Done Him Wrong* to see how the studios maintained their freedom. And West wasn't the only one kidding sex and making it profitable. Other studios had Mae Clark, Pola Negri, Jean Harlow, Ginger Rogers, and Barbara Stanwyck. But, by 1933, the censors realized that the code wasn't working and demanded that something more be done, mainly about setting some limits to sexual permissiveness on the screen.

Finally the Roman Catholic Church decided to use its power to reshape what it considered the crumbling moral dikes of America. In late 1933 the Church created the Legion of Decency. According to film historians Arthur Knight and Hollis Alpert, the legion "quickly became the most effective and disciplined pressure group the film industry had yet encountered. . . ." It still operates today under a different name. What made the legion so powerful, in addition to the fact that its values were endorsed by over fifty other religious groups of the period, was the power of the organization to successfully affect box-office receipts through bad publicity and boycotts of those films that the Church considered morally objectionable. The film industry admitted defeat. In June 1934 the code was revised, this time creating a position for the tough young Catholic reporter Joseph I. Breen, who was given power to stop any film project at any time, even after a film had been finished and distributed. His authority came through the code's new Seal of Approval. Any film not getting that seal almost automatically was refused showing in American movie theaters. Not until 1953 did anyone successfully challenge that policy. (Humorously, the film was Otto Preminger's *The Moon Is Blue*, and the Supreme Court of the United States had to rule that the use of the word "virgin" was not immoral.)

While the battle between the censors and the industry raged during 1933, West, fortunately for movie history, continued to write and make her brand of sexual comedy. For her second starring role, she chose the story of Tira, an ambitious circus dancer and lion tamer who in the end becomes a millionaire's girl friend.

I'm No Angel (1933) proved to be an even greater box-office hit than *She Done Him Wrong*, mainly because fans expected and got a delightful mixture of Westian humor and good-natured sex. By now the clever Mae had proved that the best talking-picture comedies were made by stressing wisecracks and not visual gags. *I'm No Angel*, directed by Wesley Ruggles, who came out of Sennett's film factory, contains some of her funniest material. In one scene, Tira (West) parades past a crowd of leering men remarking, "Penny for your thoughts," and then, after playing with her erotic costume adds, "Am I makin' myself clear, boys?" She then proceeds to sing "They Call Me Sister Honky-Tonk" and exits by purring, "Suckers!" Another scene has Tira discussing her horoscope. Responding to the fact that she was born in August, Tira says, "Yeah, one of the hot months." Still another scene has her exchanging romantic ideas with her millionaire boy friend, Jack Clayton (played by Cary Grant). Jack asks, "Do you mind if I get personal?" And Tira drawls, "I don't mind if you get familiar." But perhaps the most famous wisecrack in *I'm No Angel* is Tira's command to her maid (Gertrude Howard), "Beulah, peel me a grape." In short, what made the film so popular was West's theme that women had the same sexual desires as men and there was nothing wrong with them.

Exhibitors may not have agreed with Mae's advanced ideas on sexual freedom, but they loved the movies she made. They voted

West's fondness for surrounding herself with black maids
is shown here in a scene from *I'm No Angel.*
Libby Taylor is on the left; Gertrude Howard, on the right.

West one of the five best money-makers of the year in 1933 and
again in 1934. Paramount eagerly renegotiated her contract and
raised her salary to $300,000 a year, $100,000 of which went for her
screenwriting chores. By 1935, West was the highest salaried woman
in America and second (when both men and women are considered)
only to William R. Hearst. Surprisingly, her fame and fortune did
not change Mae. She still maintained that her personal life was private, refused to attend the usual Hollywood society functions, remained a non-drinker and non-smoker and spent most of her time
preparing her films.

Mae West as the fabulous Ruby Carter, who is constantly
sought after by romantic lovers like John Mack Brown (center),
a former All-American football player for the University of Alabama.
The scene is from *Belle of the Nineties* (1934).

Nevertheless, 1934 marked the start of her fall in movies. Besides
censorship, there were other problems. Her fourth film, finally released as *Belle of the Nineties,* is a good illustration. The story
focused on Ruby Carter (the typical Westian character), who dominates New Orleans' sporting world at the turn of the century and
presides over a disreputable saloon. Ruby's motto is "It is better to
be looked over than to be overlooked," and her preference for men is
limited to two kinds, domestic and foreign. She falls in love with a
boxer, Tiger Kid (Roger Pryor), and after a fixed fight, a spectac-
ular fire, and the death of the saloon's evil owner, Ruby and Tiger

get married. But the by now standard Westian story was running into difficulties. For one thing, Leo McCarey, the film's director, downplayed the plot to concentrate on individual comedy routines, editing the final print much the same way as if he were stringing together his old Laurel and Hardy shorts. Another problem had been finding a suitable leading man. Originally, Paramount had assigned George Raft the role of the Tiger Kid, but Raft refused, even risking his career by staging a walkout. The studio finally gave the role to Pryor, whose weak performance hurt West's comedy routines.

The film's greatest problem, however, came from Joseph T. Breen's department. Changes were demanded everywhere. The most ridiculous had to do with the film's title. Originally called *That St. Louis Woman*, Paramount began filming the movie under the title *It Ain't No Sin*. The publicity department, convinced that this was the final name, took a month to train fifty parrots to squawk "It Ain't No Sin," and then Paramount was forced to switch the title again, this time to *Belle of the Nineties*, putting fifty birds out of work. The more serious censorship centered on the fact that the story should not make the audience sympathetic to "crime, wrong-doing, evil or sin." The scene, for example, showing the Tiger Kid and Ruby spending the night together was cut out. Many of the more clever Westian gags were toned down or removed. And the New York censors insisted and got a marriage ceremony inserted at the film's conclusion to avoid the suggestion that Ruby and Tiger were living together out of wedlock.

The one bright spot in *Belle of the Nineties* was West's insistence that Duke Ellington and his band be hired to provide some of the movie's musical numbers. Ellington's jazz renditions and a farcical black revival meeting are used by Hollywood's bad girl to poke fun at the contrasting methods of treating good and evil.

But, in the end, Mae West was getting scrubbed and cleaned. What had been designed in her material as a sexual comedy slowly began to become a joke on the original joke, with much of the humor missing. Just how powerful the censors had become was revealed in Mae West's last four pictures for Paramount: *Goin' to Town* (1935), *Klondike Annie, Go West, Young Man,* (both made in 1936), and *Every Day's a Holiday* (1938). Her scripts were edited unmercifully.

What got past the Hays office during pre-production got cut during the editing stages and even after the movies were released to the public. No West film better illustrated her dilemma than did *Klondike Annie*.

Directed by the legendary Hollywood director Raoul Walsh, *Klondike Annie* was Mae West's last try to please the killjoys and still create great comedy. The movie also reflected her strong religious feelings, which surfaced during the thirties. Focusing on Rose Carlton, known as the Frisco Doll (West), the plot follows Rose's rescue from poverty by the sinister Chan Lo (Harold Huber); she then becomes his mistress. Soon tired of her sordid existence, Rose tries to escape, but Chan finds out and, in the fight that follows, Rose kills him. In order to avoid arrest by the San Francisco police, she takes a boat that is bound for the Yukon and captained by her new love interest, Bull Brackett (Victor McLaglen). During the passage north, Rose becomes friendly with passenger Sister Annie Alden (Helen Jerome Eddy), and the two discuss the sister's mission to help the unfortunate, starving men in the frozen north. Sister Annie dies, however, before the boat reaches Alaska. At first, Rose disguises herself as the missionary to avoid detection, but later becomes a reformed woman and decides to carry on the dead sister's work.

The first half of the movie had all the Westian style, complete with songs and double entendres. But as soon as Rose meets Sister Annie, the dialogue and the plot take on a more serious tone and one gets the feeling of being lectured at from the screen. Seen from today's perspective, *Klondike Annie* is a self-conscious comedy attacking hypocrisy and greed. But in 1936 the censors were blind to any of West's virtues. For example, the hypocritical Hearst, who for over twenty-five years had openly maintained both a wife and mistress, professed shock at West's use of religious material and wrote editorials in his thirty-five newspapers about the need to put a stop to Mae West. He even refused to let his papers carry ads for *Klondike Annie*. The Breen office did its share as well, forcing cuts in the finished film, the best known being the deletion of the scene where Rose dresses up the dead missionary as a prostitute to fool the police. Even *The New York Times* commented in its review, "It's downright discouraging to hear Miss West perplex Mr. McLaglen by saying that she was 'heading for the arms of Morpheus' and it is worse when McLaglen remarks, 'I can always tell a lady when I see one' and she comes back with a 'Yeah! What do you tell 'em.' If that is what the Legion of Decency meant when it rated 'Annie' as objectionable in part, then we agree with the Legion." No wonder artists like Fields and West rarely listened to critical advice.

The Paramount bad girl didn't help her problems any by appearing the following year on Edgar Bergen and Charlie McCarthy's radio show. December 12, 1937, was a Sunday night that radio executives did not let Mae forget for the next twelve years. Doing a skit written by the sponsor's publicity agency, Mae played a frustrated Eve trying to force a lazy Adam (Don Ameche), whom she referred to as "Tall, Dark, and Lukewarm," to break his lease in the Garden of Eden. The protests over what now is seen as a very mild spoof (the entire routine is available on Mark 56 records) reached epic proportions, and West was not allowed back on the airwaves until the end of the forties.

By 1938, Paramount was convinced that their controversial star was box-office poison. Not only had she angered the censors, but there was also a growing indication that many females in the audience were annoyed by the mockery that Hollywood had made of women. Although that anti-West image still persists among some women today, feminist critics are defending the star as one of the most original artists of her times. Joan Mellen, for example, in her book *Women and Their Sexuality in the New Film*, sums up the modern position: "West was the *auteur* of films redolent with wit in which the punchline always went to the women. It should not be forgotten that she worked in a medium devoted to glorifying male prowess and female incapacity. And it took courage in its time . . . to present Hollywood with a reversal of roles and a manifest contempt for the culture which had for so long demeaned the capacities of women." Nevertheless, Paramount, in 1938, refused to produce West's screenplay on Catherine the Great, and she left the studio which a few years back she had saved from oblivion.

Universal Pictures, however, was in the midst of a rebuilding program and contracted the aging star to write a spoof on Hollywood's recent cowboy movies. The film was *My Little Chickadee*

No movie West ever made caused as great a stir as *Klondike Annie* (1936).
Shown here as the fugitive Rose Carlton,
she befriends a sickly missionary (Helen Jerome Eddy).

(1940) and starred both West and W. C. Fields. (After some arguing, Fields got permission to include some of his own material.) Mae
always had very mixed feelings about W.C. On the one hand, she
hated his drinking and high-handed ways, and even had written into
her contract that he would be thrown off the set if she found him
drinking. (Fields devised all sorts of schemes to fool her, but got
caught once, according to Hollywood legend, and screamed that
someone had taken the cork out of his lunch as West had him
ejected from the set for that day.) On the other hand, she pitied
the fact that such a great comedian had destroyed himself through

Her film career destroyed by the Breen office,
West tried to recapture her hold on movie audiences by teaming up
for one time only with Fields in a spoof on the Hollywood Westerns.
The film was *My Little Chickadee* (1940).

alcohol. Anyone viewing the film comes away with a sense of her kindness in providing him with the best gags.

The story itself dealt with Flower Belle Lee (West), who is run out of one town after another and, as a result, enters into a marriage of convenience with a traveling con man by the name of Cuthbert J. Twillie (Fields). Except for a few short but funny scenes, the two stars rarely appear together on the screen. Probably one of the few good lines in the film comes when the two clowns are discussing their relations with each other and Twillie wants to know more about his bride. She replies that there is nothing good she can say about herself and he responds, "I can see what's good. Tell me the rest."

Despite the film's strong showing at the box office, West never made another picture for Universal. She went back on the stage, eventually got the famous Mike Todd to produce her play *Catherine the Great*, and spent most of the next thirty years of her life touring with revivals of her old shows. At other times, mainly in the fifties, West put together a satirical nightclub act in which she was worshiped by eight musclemen clothed in loin cloths.

But not once in all that time was she ever forgotten. The British pilots in World War II, for example, named a lifejacket after her, the "Mae West." Nor, for that matter, did she ever tone down her comic style. In 1959 she thrilled viewers of the annual Academy Awards show with a marvelous skit with Rock Hudson, and then months later so annoyed the television executives at CBS that they canceled her taped interview on the "Person-to-Person" program, fearing that her answers were just too suggestive for American viewers. As recently as 1970 when 20th Century-Fox produced its disastrous movie *Myra Breckinridge*, the studio paid Mae West a half million dollars to appear in a small role and gave her, not the star, Raquel Welch, top billing.

Still active today after more than three-quarters of a century in show business, the remarkable woman remains an example of what great comedy is all about. She tried to destroy the conventions of an age that refused to be changed. As Mae West puts it, "I'm a girl who lost her reputation and never missed it."

THE LUNATIC CLOWNS

THE
MARX
BROTHERS

In thinking back to the days of Fields and West, we can see one conclusion clearly. For all its faults—and there were many—Hollywood in the thirties had superb comedians. Never again would funny people be so numerous in movies. Part of their appeal was their ability to do on screen what we dared not do in our everyday lives. They gave in to their emotions. They rebelled against misused authority. They ridiculed middle-class myths. To them, money and property and position meant corruption and abuse and compromise. No matter what the film, these great clowns hammered out the same philosophy: expose pretension and champion the average person. The list of the fabulous Hollywood comics of the thirties was long and honorable, but at the top stood the Marx Brothers.

The obvious question is "Why?" What made the sons of a magician's daughter the most enduring comics of their time? One theory is that the Marx Brothers' comedies were the best-constructed movies. Although Fields and West, for example, were first-rate clowns, their ability to conceive and to execute film ideas was limited. Not so with the Marx Brothers, who had superb writers and worked for outstanding producers. Another theory is that they were more ambitious than other clowns in their assault on society. True enough that Fields took on middle-class myths, while West demolished sexual taboos, but the Marxes confronted America itself. Nothing was safe from their mockery: education, politics, business, democracy, government, sex, culture, war, medicine, high society, old-world ties, and the law. Still another theory is that the characters the brothers played on screen symbolized all that we hate about urban society. Groucho embodied the nasty, double-talking city slicker; Chico, the immigrant schemer with the horrible puns; and Harpo, the silent insane tramp ready to attack at a moment's notice. The brothers turned their strange characters into heroes ready to expose the high and the mighty, and we loved them for it.

Perhaps the most fascinating theory is that offered by surrealists. Concerned with radically overthrowing all existing social, scientific, and philosophical values, the surrealists praise the Marx Brothers as great liberators of our imagination. In a Marx film, traditional values are held in contempt. Instead of being intimidated by society, the comedians do as they wish and make anarchy seem marvelous. Their comic assault on reality, so the surrealist theory argues, turns the Marx Brothers into gadflies. Their actions force us to rethink what is logical and reasonable in our everyday lives. Comedians like Harpo and Groucho, therefore, emerge as subversive individuals protesting against our drab existence, urging us to give in to our innermost desires.

But theories come and go. What has remained constant for the past forty-five years is the public's loyalty. And probably the best answer to the question of their enduring popularity is very simple: they remain incredibly funny men.

Like the other great clowns of the talkies, the Marxes did not become overnight sensations. They spent more than a quarter of a century developing their comic gifts in vaudeville and musical revues before making their first successful film in 1929. To understand what made them so good, we first need to consider their roots.

The story really begins in Germany, where the Schoenbergs and their children—Minnie, Hannah, and Al—spent years traveling about the countryside. Poppa Schoenberg was a ventriloquist and magician who performed at local fairs, while his wife followed the act with music on the harp so that audiences could dance. But in the latter part of the nineteenth century anti-Semitism was rising and, as a result, the Schoenberg family emigrated to America. To support their by now elderly parents, Minnie became a seamstress in a straw-hat factory on Manhattan's Upper East Side, while Al found work as a pants presser. But Al couldn't hold a job, mainly because he preferred singing to pressing. So Minnie decided that her brother should follow the family tradition and go into show business. She briefly became his agent and, not too long afterward, he changed his name to Shean and rose in the vaudeville ranks to become one of the most famous entertainers of the day, in a team known as Gallagher and Shean. Minnie, in the meantime, fell in love and married another Jewish immigrant named Sam Marx, a tailor like none other. Sam bragged that he could size up a customer just by looking at him; tape measurements were unnecessary. His judgment in such matters was about as accurate as President Hoover's predictions about the Depression. After seeing the results of his work, very few of Sam's customers paid him, let alone ordered another suit. As a result, the newlyweds found themselves constantly in debt. Eventually they moved into a flat on Ninety-third Street and Third Avenue, where poverty was so widespread that their condition seemed commonplace. And it was here that the Marxes started their next generation.

First came Leonard (Chico), who was born on March 22, 1887. Most of his childhood was divided between pool halls and pawnshops. That is, until he discovered girls, and then he hardly had time to sleep. It was a pattern that he followed religiously until his death seventy-four years later. The second son was Adolph, later changed to Arthur (Harpo), born on November 23, 1888. Of all the brothers, he was the most loved. Harpo[1] was known for his kindness and his gentle nature. He also accepted life as it was, except on his bar mitzvah. That was the day he received a watch, which he knew would soon be pawned by his older brother unless Harpo did something clever. It was not that he objected to Chico "borrowing" to pay his frequent gambling debts; he just loved his new watch. So he calmly took the hands off the dial, ensuring that the now unpawnable watch would be his forever. The third son, Julius (Groucho), arrived on October 2, 1890. He made it a lifelong ambition to be different from the other members of the family. If they loved gambling, Groucho considered it a bore. If they quit school as soon as possible (Harpo never even passed the second grade), he stayed as long as he could. But few people in the early part of the twentieth century ever went beyond high school, and Groucho wasn't one of them. Where the other brothers had little ambition, he longed to be a doctor. Where they tried to squeeze every bit of fun out of life, Groucho always worried and criticized and envied. Nevertheless, it was the striking differences in personalities among the three older Marxes which later helped form the basis of their remarkable comedy. The same could not be said of Minnie's other sons, neither of whom ever became a big name in show business. The fourth son, Milton (Gummo), was born in 1892. Although he had the usual family interest in card playing and good times, Gummo realized early in life that he preferred a normal routine divorced from the

[1]Although the Marx boys did not get their famous names until 1914, it seems best to use them early in the chapter to avoid any unnecessary confusion.

Following a successful vaudeville matinee,
the then unknown Marx family poses for a family picture.
From left to right: Harpo, Chico, Sam Marx (father), Zeppo,
Minnie Marx (mother), Gummo, and Groucho.

hectic life of an actor. The last of the brothers was Herbert (Zeppo), born in 1901. Considered by some Marx biographers to have been offstage the funniest member of the family, Herbert never really found a place for himself in the family tradition. The youngest Marx always felt frustrated around his brothers. He wanted to be like them, but never seemed able to do much about his dreams.

Conditions in the Marx household by 1902 didn't appear promising for anyone. There was very little money coming into the twenty-seven-dollar-a-month flat on Ninety-third Street, which now housed ten people (the five brothers, their parents, their maternal grandparents, and an adopted sister). The problem was what to do for food and rent.

Then Minnie decided on a solution. She would do for her children what she had done for her brother. She would make them vaudeville stars. The only question was which son to launch first.

The "Napoleon Scene" from *I'll Say She Is* (1924).
In examining the picture years later, Harpo remarked
that not only didn't he know what the scene was about, he didn't
even know what the show's title meant. That's how crazy the act was.
From left to right: Harpo, Chico, Lotta Miles, Groucho, and Zeppo.

Chico, being the oldest, was the natural choice. A piano was purchased and music lessons arranged. Harpo wanted to learn too, but Minnie had enough trouble just finding money for the piano and Chico's lessons. So Harpo stood by and watched his older brother learn the keyboard. Afterward, when no one was around, he practiced what he had observed. Chico, as you might expect, progressed much faster than Harpo. Before long, he was good enough to find work as a musician, playing the piano at the local saloons and silent-movie houses. Such jobs, however, rarely held his interest. Whenever he got word of a card game, Chico disappeared from work. To ensure that his family still benefited from his jobs, he took advantage of the fact that the youthful Harpo looked almost like his twin. Most employers of the day couldn't tell them apart—at first. As a result, Chico found the jobs and stayed around for a few days; after that, Harpo took over. The plan had one flaw—Harpo could play only two songs. Even the dumbest boss recognized the switch in piano players after a week and the boys would be on the lookout for another sucker. Thus the responsibility for being the first Marx brother to break into show business fell on the middle son, Groucho.

Despite the fact that he had a good soprano voice for a four-teen-year-old, Groucho wasn't thrilled with the idea. He preferred his books to the stage. But Minnie remained firm. His first part was in a Gus Edwards' musical, *The Messenger Boys*, a local group organized to act as fund raisers for the victims of the 1906 San Francisco earthquake. Following that brief stint, Groucho answered an ad in the New York *Morning World*: "Boy Singer Wanted for Touring Vaudeville Act." He got the job and became a female impersonator in a second-rate trio headed by a con man who soon left the fifteen-year-old Marx stranded and penniless in Cripple Creek, Colorado. The unhappy incident didn't faze Minnie at all. She wired her son money to get home and lined up another job. This time Groucho sang alongside an English lady who shortly thereafter fell in love with a lion tamer on the bill. Eventually, the two lovers ran off together, once more leaving the Marx kid stranded.

Obviously, this could not continue. So the unflappable Minnie decided to give the problem of her children's success in vaudeville her full attention. Furthermore, she decided to team her fourth son, Gummo, with Groucho and bill the kids as a duet. The two boys had nothing to say about the matter. Acting as their agent, Minnie began hounding the big-time booking agencies, hardly the place to start with such an inexperienced duet. But Minnie aimed high for her sons. When nothing else worked, she managed to get the bookers to her home where Sam, now known as "Frenchie" because of his fancy dress and elegant cooking, created sumptuous meals for his guests. Afterward, he hosted a first-rate pinochle game, and bookers, out of gratitude or shame, found work for the Marx kids.

The duet became known in the business as a "number two act."

That is, they performed on stage at the start of the bill, just as the audience was wandering in for the evening's entertainment. Normally, it made no difference what number two act was booked; one was as bad as another. The Marxes, however, were worse than most.

As bookings became more difficult, the optimistic Minnie enlarged the act and decided to put some spice into it. She advertised for a gorgeous female singer, but had to settle for an attractive girl with a glass eye who always sang off key. To make matters worse, the girl was also a nymphomaniac, which even the brothers reluctantly felt was more than the act could take. Before long, the girl was out and a male vocalist put in her place. Known as "The Three Nightingales," the trio bored audiences for most of 1909.

But by 1910 their reputation was so bad that Minnie once more decided to enlarge the act. One reason was that bookers paid more money if the act had more people. Secondly, and more important, Minnie wanted to keep her sons together, and she felt the time was right for Harpo to go onstage. So one day, quite unexpectedly, Minnie appeared at the hotel where her son was working as a bellhop, and as Harpo described the event:

She collared me, dragged me to the cab, took me to the small theater [Henderson's Coney Island] where Groucho and Gummo were appearing, and literally shoved me on stage.

Naturally, I had no experience, no instruction, only a sense of complete confusion. But I stood there, dumb as a telephone pole, while Groucho and Gummo ad-libbed me into the act.

He added elsewhere:

With my first look at my first audience, I reverted to being a boy again. My reaction was instantaneous and overwhelming. I wet my pants.

And thus "The Four Nightingales" was born. The act was no better than the previous Marx attempts, and within months bookers fled at the sight of Minnie.

Feeling she had "exhausted" the New York area, the stage-door mother moved her family to Chicago, where competition wasn't as great and her boys could get a fresh start. It was a good idea.

These were the days when Chicago was the hub of small-time vaudeville and an excellent training ground for would-be comedians. There were many reasons why. First of all, a newcomer got a chance to work with older and more experienced performers. Standing in the wings, the neophyte could pick up tips about timing, different comedy styles, and maybe even steal some material for his own act. Secondly, a newcomer was taught flexibility. No show was ever really the same night after night. Within any given week you'd be performing in a theater, at conventions, picnics, and amusement parks, as well as playing benefits and stags. Third, a newcomer couldn't afford to be bad. In addition to being fired by the management and having your bookings canceled en route across the country, a bad actor faced the instantaneous wrath of rough customers who paid for a night's entertainment. If you didn't provide it in some way, you were bombarded with rotten fruit, tobacco juice, spitballs, eggs, or anything else at hand.

Imagine how hard life was for a bad act like the Four Nightingales. According to Harpo in his autobiography, *Harpo Speaks*:

We had to brazen our way into small towns in the Midwest and down South, where we had three strikes against us. One: we were stage folks, in a class with gypsies and other vagrants. Two: we were Jewish. Three: we had New York accents. And well—strike four: the Four Nightingales weren't very good.

Over the next few years, however, poverty and small-time vaudeville began to shape their abilities much as they had for Chaplin and Fields.

To amuse themselves, the quartet developed into a roughhouse act. In other words, they became unpredictable onstage. At any unannounced moment and for no apparent reason, the boys would start kicking, slapping, and fighting with each other. This crude form of slapstick comedy amused no one but themselves. That was all right with the Marx Brothers. If Minnie was determined to make them into actors, they intended to enjoy themselves. It was a principle the brothers held to for the rest of their careers—doing exactly what they wanted to do, whenever they wanted to do it.

When the Four Nightingales had worn out their welcome,

The Marx Brothers in their first successful movie,
Cocoanuts (1929).

Minnie and her sister Hannah joined the act and billed the group as "The Six Mascots." By 1914, however, bookers had come to the conclusion that a Marx act by any name was worth avoiding. Then came the night in Nacogdoches, Texas.

Right in the middle of the Mascots' act, the audience bolted from the theater to watch the capture of a runaway mule. When the customers returned to their seats, the irate Marx Brothers decided to turn their roughhouse humor on the audience and began ad-libbing wisecracks about Nacogdoches. The surprise was that the local crowd loved it. In fact, the ad-libbing became so talked about that a nearby theater owner from Denison came backstage one night and offered the act a special booking at a fine salary for the weekend. There was

As the stock market was crumbling, the Marx Brothers
were making their second film hit, *Animal Crackers* (1930).
Margaret Dumont plays the confused hostess Mrs. Rittenhouse (right).

one catch. The Denison manager wanted the Marxes to do two
different shows: the Mascot act on Friday night and a comedy show
on Saturday night. Minnie assured him they could do it.

Once the deal had been accepted and the man left the dressing
room, the boys exploded. They had no comedy act and how did
Minnie expect them to put one together in a few days? The argument went on for a while, until someone came up with the idea of
a school routine, similar to the material that Gus Edwards and his
imitators had been doing in vaudeville for years. After all, the Denison audience were going to be the members of a teachers' convention and would love some classroom comedy. The more the family
talked, the more confident they became. Since Groucho was the

"thinker" in the group, he got the part of the teacher. All he needed
for a costume was his uncle's frock coat, a pair of glasses, and a fake
mustache. The rest of the group would be his students, with Harpo
featured as the Patsy Brannigan type, the country bumpkin with the
crazy faces. It was an obvious choice since Harpo, for years, had been
imitating the facial expressions of a New York cigar-maker named
Gookie. As a kid, Harpo had studied Mr. Gookie's facial contortions
when the man became absorbed in his work. "His tongue," wrote
Harpo in 1961, "lolled out in a fat roll, his cheeks puffed out, and his
eyes popped out and crossed themselves." In addition to playing
"Gookie," Harpo agreed to wear a handmade wig that Aunt Hannah
had created out of cotton and old rope. And thus began the formal
stage career of the Marx Brothers as comedians.

The comedy show itself was divided into two parts. Act One was
entitled "Fun in Hi Skule" and portrayed the difficulties in educating
the uneducable. Act Two, "Mr. Green's Reception," offered a class
reunion many years later. The best material appeared in the first act
with the spirited students and their ad-libbing teacher. Typical of
"Fun in Hi Skule" was the teacher asking Gummo, "If you had ten
apples and wanted to divide them among six people, what would
you do?" His quick reply: "Make applesauce." Or the famous exchange between Groucho and Harpo:

> *Teacher: What is the shape of the world?*
> *Harpo: I don't know.*
> *Teacher: Well, what shape are my cufflinks?*
> *Harpo: Square.*
> *Teacher: Not my weekday cufflinks, the ones I wear on Sundays.*
> *Harpo: Oh! Round.*
> *Teacher: Okay, what is the shape of the world?*
> *Harpo: Square on weekdays, round on Sundays.*

And this was how the act proceeded, from one gag to another, more
like a Ping-Pong match than a well-disciplined stage routine. That is,
until the group reached the Barrison Theater in Waukegan, Illinois.

Minutes after the curtain went up on "Fun in Hi Skule"
Groucho interrupted the standard gags and began making wisecracks
about the piano player in the orchestra. Once Harpo saw who the

piano player was, he joined in. The musician, of course, was Chico, whom Minnie had convinced to give up his successful career as a song plugger and to join the family onstage. Interestingly, that same night in the theater orchestra was a youngster by the name of Benny Kubelsky, who had gotten permission from the local musician's union to play the fiddle. Minnie invited the clever boy to join the tour, but he was too young. Soon after, he started out on his own and became a superb comedian, using the name of Jack Benny.

Meanwhile, for the first time, the three Marx Brothers were together and starting to develop the comic characters that would eventually bring them to stardom. Groucho worked on his illogical speeches and fast ad-libbing; Harpo worked on his funny faces and unpredictable gags; and Chico, because of his flair for dialects and bad puns, perfected the role of the scheming immigrant. The brothers' flair for roughhouse comedy and their striking personalities began to make an impression on out-of-the-way towns.

Back in Chicago, however, their comedy act laid an egg. Critics complimented the brothers, but complained bitterly about their material. It was 1914 and Minnie had tried for many years on her own to do something for her sons, but now she needed help. Uncle Al was sent for. One look at his nephews onstage convinced him that their critics were right. In the past he had recommended that they pay writers to create material for them, but each time the material had proven inadequate. Minnie pleaded with her brother to write the boys an act himself. And so, late one night, according to legend, Al Shean, using a butcher's brown wrapping paper, wrote a skit entitled "Home Again."

More than anything else, "Home Again" was a musical revue with an assortment of singers, dancers, and Marx Brothers comedy. Groucho played himself, the king of the ad-lib. But Uncle Al had forgotten to consider the egos of Harpo and Chico. When Harpo saw that he had been given only three lines in the entire forty-minute revue, he complained. Thinking quickly, Uncle Al said he agreed that this was very wrong. So he took out the three lines and persuaded Harpo to play the part of the traditional silent clown, much in the fashion of the great French pantomimists. Harpo liked the idea, and never again spoke onstage. Uncle Al then turned to Chico and pointed

After making two films in Long Island, the Marx Brothers moved
to Hollywood and made their first original film *Monkey Business* (1931).
Harpo's wild expression is directed toward retired gangster
Joe Helton (played by Rockliffe Fellowes).

out that since the oldest Marx had such a knack for doing Italian
dialects, Chico should write his own material. In those days, no one
considered such a characterization ethnically offensive. As Groucho
said later, "Who knew from ethnic unbalance in our day? We were
just struggling vaudevillians trying to be funny. Dialect comics were
very popular when we started out, so we decided to make Chico a
Wop." The final touch came when Harpo became jealous of the name
Chico was making for himself as a pistol-playing piano player (Chico
accented his notes by punching the keys with his second finger),
and insisted he be allowed to play his grandmother's harp in the act.
Minnie couldn't find her mother's harp, so she bought her son a
used one, and Harpo taught himself some songs and was happy.

Only years later did he discover that he had learned to play the harp incorrectly, but by then his technique had become world-famous and professionals wanted to study with him and not the other way around.

It was while the boys were touring with "Home Again" that they met a clever vaudevillian named Art Fisher, whose favorite pastime was making wisecracks about a comic-strip character named "Knocko the Monk." One night, so the story goes, the boys and Fisher were in a card game, and as Fisher dealt the cards around the table, he coined a new name for each brother. To Milton, who loved gumsole shoes, he gave the name "Gummo." To Julius, the fusspot of the family, he gave the name "Groucho." To Lenny, who loved to chase the girls (in those days known as "chickens"), "Chicko." (It was only later when his name was misspelled that it became "Chico.") And, of course, Arthur became "Harpo."

When the United States went to war in 1917, Gummo was the only son to serve (the other brothers, except for the underaged Herbert, proved unfit for military service). At that point, Minnie insisted that her youngest son take Gummo's place in "Home Again," mainly as a straight man. For no apparent reason, the Marxes named their kid brother "Zeppo," and the act continued. Following the war, Gummo's decision to quit show business made Zeppo a fixture in what was now widely regarded as a "lunatic" act.

Nine years after they had left New York, the Marx Brothers came back. Only this time, the rugged life of boardinghouses, railroad stations, one-night stands, and tough audiences had changed them. The boys were ready for big-time vaudeville. And, for a while, they did well. They even played the Palace, the top of the vaudeville ladder.

By 1922 the Marx Brothers had developed their famous images. Groucho, for example, had taken to smoking a cigar onstage, mainly because it served as a safeguard when he was stuck for a joke. By taking a long puff on his cigar, Groucho not only got a laugh, but also found time to think of a good line. He had also taken to wearing a black grease-paint mustache, the result of his having arrived late one night for an opening curtain and discovering that his quickly painted on mustache was funnier than the crepe one he had been using. Harpo had also expanded his image. He now appeared onstage in a battered plug hat on top of his handmade wig. Included as well were a dirty raincoat, clashing plaid and polka dot ties and shirts, and baggy pants held up by a rope belt. Since Harpo didn't speak onstage, he made himself understood by making weird faces, honking on a horn, blowing bubbles, and whistling. What's more, Harpo had created a gag whereby he had things hidden under his raincoat and at the appropriate moment began dropping knives from his sleeves or pulling out blowtorches when someone asked for a light. Taken together, the Marx Brothers appeared as lunatics let loose on society.

Just when the Marxes thought there was no stopping them, they had a run-in over their antics with the czars of big-time vaudeville: the Keith-Albee syndicate. The order went out from Albee himself to ban the roughhouse comics from the major vaudeville theaters and circuits. It looked as if the Marxes had blown their big chance. In a desperate attempt to stay in the East, the brothers went into musical revues, but one show after another flopped. By 1923 everyone seemed discouraged but Chico. Then, once more, came a lucky break.

Chico, through his gambling, had become friendly with Tom Johnstone, a composer, whose brother had just failed in a show-business venture with a small-time independent producer named Joseph M. Gaites. In conversation, Chico discovered that Gaites had been asked by a businessman who owned a theater in Philadelphia to mount a show with a role for his mistress. Gaites, sensing that this was a great chance to unload his expensive scenery from the closed Johnstone revue, desperately wanted a show, any show. His concern was in turning a quick profit. In short, Chico convinced all the parties involved that the Marx Brothers were the answer to their problems.

The Johnstone brothers quickly went to work on their ailing musical, bringing the material into line with the Marxes' sense of humor, and by late spring *I'll Say She Is* opened at Philadelphia's Walnut Street Theatre. Despite the show's smashing success, it did not reach Broadway until almost a year later, and then only because the Marxes threatened to quit unless they played New York.

Getting to Broadway was one thing; staying there was something else. Once before the brothers had made the big time, only to fall from favor and face obscurity. The feeling this time was if they didn't succeed, they were washed up, and it looked as if the odds were against them. The tough New York critics who determined the fate of Broadway shows had heard that *I'll Say She Is* was a low-budget production. Consequently, they had decided to see another, more expensive show scheduled to open the same night. That would mean almost no announcement of the new Marx revue and thus certain failure. To add to the family's troubles, Minnie broke her leg trying on a new dress.

Then came opening night—May 19, 1924—and once more Lady Luck stepped in. The big show scheduled to open was postponed thereby freeing the critics to attend, however reluctantly, *I'll Say She Is*. So, as Minnie was being carried to her seat, in walked such famous writers as Alexander Woollcott, George S. Kaufman, Heywood Broun, George Jean Nathan, and Herman Mankiewicz. Once the curtain went up, no one stopped laughing for more than two hours, and at the very material vaudeville audiences had only recently considered old hat. After the show the powerful drama critics competed with one another in their reviews to see who could praise the Marx Brothers most.

The next morning found Minnie's boys big stars. Woollcott, probably the most influential critic in America for a quarter of a century, pronounced Harpo a brilliant clown and personally made him a member of the most famous circle of wits in the country: the Thanatopsis Upper West Side Inside Straight and Literary Club. Housed at Manhattan's Algonquin Hotel, the group included, among others, Woollcott (the acknowledged leader), Kaufman, Robert Benchley, Heywood Broun, Marc Connelly, and the future founder of *The New Yorker* magazine (published for the first time on February 1, 1925), Harold Ross. These were only a few of the friends that surrounded the Marxes from then on. In future years, the list of writers friendly to the brothers would also include George Bernard Shaw, William Somerset Maugham, and T. S. Eliot.

But the problem facing the brothers in 1925 was how to follow up the success of their last show. The decision was turned over to Broadway producer Sam Harris, the former partner of George M.

Cohan. Everyone agreed that a strong script was needed, and that there was only one man clever enough to do the job, George S. Kaufman. The critic now turned playwright would in later years pen the first Pulitzer Prize musical, *Of Thee I Sing*, as well as the delightful *You Can't Take It With You*. The idea of writing a show for the Marxes, however, hardly appealed to him. He reportedly exclaimed, "Are you crazy? *Write* a show for the Marx Brothers? I'd rather write a show for the Barbary apes!" It wasn't that he didn't love the boys. He just felt they were lunatics who never studied their parts, never used their lines, and always missed rehearsals. But Harris won Kaufman over and, with the music of a young composer named Irving Berlin, a show was put together.

Harris also did the Marxes another major favor. He introduced them to Margaret Dumont, probably one of the greatest straight ladies of that or any time. She, too, had her problems with the Marxes. Although Dumont adored the clowns and rarely worked with anyone else for the rest of her life, she absolutely did not understand their comedy. Furthermore, they made her life miserable during performances, pulling chairs out from under her, frightening her with small animals, and goosing her whenever the opportunity arose. To her credit, she always came back for more.

On December 8, 1925, *The Cocoanuts* opened at Broadway's Lyric Theatre, and the Marxes were a smash hit. The loosely based plot had Groucho managing a 600-room hotel while at the same time trying to pull off a big real estate swindle. As usual, the other brothers popped in and out of the thin story, doing their specialties whenever the spirit moved them.

Their reputations as lunatic comedians now added to their box-office success. People came to see the show several times, realizing that no two performances were ever the same. Legend has it that one evening backstage, Kaufman stopped talking, walked to the wings, listened for a moment, and then said, "I think I heard one of my lines." But the most memorable story from the show was the gag Harpo pulled one night. Determined to throw Groucho's timing off, Harpo convinced one of the chorus girls to run across the stage, screaming, so that he could chase her and upset Groucho. Instead of getting flustered, Groucho won the battle of wits by taking out his

Harpo does his best to unnerve the scheming Miss Bailey
(Thelma Todd) in the Marx Brothers' 1932 movie *Horsefeathers*.

watch and commenting, "The nine-twenty's on time." Later on, Harpo found himself in trouble backstage. The chorus girl he had so carelessly selected was the girl friend of the gangster Legs Diamond, who didn't like the idea. So Harpo quickly found a substitute, and kept the blonde-chasing routine with him for the rest of his professional career.

Perhaps the most significant aspect of *The Cocoanuts* was the influence Kaufman exerted on the Marxes. In later years Groucho credited the playwright with developing the highly creative way that the brothers treated the American language. One of the best examples in the play occurs when Groucho quells a bellhop mutiny over past wages. "Do you want to be wage slaves?" he asks, and then goes on to say, "Of course not. Well, what makes wage slaves? Wages. I want you to be free. Remember there's nothing like *Liberty*, except *Collier's* and *The Saturday Evening Post*. Be free, my friends. One for all and all for me—me for you and three for five and six for a quarter." This illogical progression of deductive unreasoning became the typical Marx trademark in all future shows and films, usually highlighting the exchanges between Groucho and Chico.

In 1928, Sam Harris produced the last Marx revue, *Animal Crackers*, written by Kaufman in collaboration with Morrie Ryskind. The show's music was composed by the clever team of Bert Kalmar and Harry Ruby (their lives were dramatized in the 1950 M-G-M musical *Three Little Words*). Once again, the thin plot acted as a pretext for getting the Marxes onstage. This time the story had the wealthy Mrs. Rittenhouse (Dumont) throwing a swanky affair to mark the debut of a famous painting, which is first stolen and then recovered. High on her guest list were the famous African explorer, Captain Jeffrey Spaulding (Groucho), his assistant (Zeppo), Signor Emanuel Ravelli (Chico), and the weird Professor (Harpo). The Marxes were never better, and the fast pace of their wisecracks, puns, and roughhouse gags prompted Benchley to describe them as "cheerful maniacs."

Following the opening of *Animal Crackers* on October 23, 1928, the brothers seemed on top of the world. They were big stars, and were making a fortune in the stock market. These were the circumstances when Paramount Pictures signed them to a movie contract for three films at $75,000 per film. The first movie was a film version of *The Cocoanuts.*

The conditions under which that movie was made were incredible. To begin with, the Marxes refused to rehearse. They had done the play for three years, were making the movie version at the same time they were appearing on Broadway in *Animal Crackers,* and spent most of their time pursuing their individual fancies: Chico gambling; Harpo chasing girls; and Groucho worrying about everything. Once before Groucho and Harpo had appeared in a movie (1920), and the results were so bad that Groucho feared the team might fail again. Paramount didn't make things any easier. The studio assigned the directing chores to Robert Florey, a Frenchman (later famous for his horror films) who didn't speak English and couldn't understand the Marxes' sense of humor. Throughout the weeks of shooting, he kept asking, "This is funny?"

What wasn't funny to Florey was riotous to the film's technicians. Without rehearsals, the camera crew didn't know where to place the immobile, new, sound cameras. Between laughing at the Marx gags and being unable to follow their jumping and running around, the cameramen had a tough time getting a good picture, while the soundmen found it difficult to record the Marx wisecracks. One scene in particular caused nightmares. Groucho and Chico did a bit involving a large map, but every time they opened the map, the paper sounded as if a bomb had gone off. Finally, after twenty-seven retakes, someone got the bright idea to soak the map in water so it wouldn't make any noise. All in all, the completed film provides a fascinating record of how difficult it was in 1929 to film a Marx Brothers musical.

Even with the technical flaws, the film version of *The Cocoanuts* is delightful, and audiences today can recognize the basic Marx characterizations. There is Groucho, with his energetic, rich speech patterns, reasoning illogically but somehow achieving a respected position in society. Into his realm come Chico and Harpo, stupid and lovable creatures who look for any opportunity to ridicule and subvert the world around them. And then there is Dumont, the stately, dignified, rich matron who ignores Chico, is amused by Groucho, and is concerned about Harpo's mental health. Throughout the film she continues to inquire about Harpo's behavior, "What's the matter with him *now?*" Here, too, in their first major film is the formula for all future Marx Brothers classics: food, drink, music, games, and money. These ingredients mixed together became their stock comedy material.

Unfortunately for the Marx family, 1929 did not end the way it began. Just as the brothers were preparing to do a national tour of *Animal Crackers*, Minnie died. It seemed as if she had worked all her life to make her sons stars and, now that her dream had come true, she could bow out. In his tribute to her, Woollcott summed up the family's feelings: "Minnie Marx was a wise, tolerant, generous, gallant matriarch. . . . She was in this world sixty-five years and *lived* all sixty-five of them." To add to the brothers' unhappiness, the stock market crashed and wiped out all of the family's finances. The one exception was Chico, who had lost his money each week betting on the horses. As 1930 approached, the one bright spot in their lives was the fact that they were still earning a living, which was more than millions of Americans could say.

The film version of *Animal Crackers* (1930) turned out to be an improvement over their first Paramount venture. One reason was the unusual tactics of its director, Victor Heerman. Learning from Florey's problems, Heerman demanded that cages be built on the studio set, and he personally placed each Marx in one, together with an individual keeper. In this way Heerman knew where to find the brothers when he needed them. The idea worked; the film appears to have been carefully rehearsed, as the gags and visual humor are crisp and well-timed. Many critics, in fact, consider Groucho's performance as Captain Spaulding his best, starting with his being carried in by African bearers and complaining, "What? From Africa to here, $1.85? That's an outrage. I told you not to take me through Australia . . ." to his final exchange with Chico when the two try to solve the case of the missing painting and he exclaims, "You solved it. The credit is all yours. The painting was eaten by a left-handed moth." The movie also provides viewers with an almost complete visual catalogue of Harpo's famous routines, ending with a delightful display of his coat trick.

By 1931 the Marxes had grown tired of their stage careers. For

Chico and Groucho also take turns attacking Miss Todd
in this musical-comedy romance about college life.

more than twenty-five years they had been working six days a week,
and now movies gave them a chance to work for a concentrated period of time and then relax before the next performance. So the
brothers moved West. Over the next two years, they made three
more Paramount films: *Monkey Business* (1931), *Horsefeathers*
(1932), and *Duck Soup* (1933). The first two ridiculed the gangster-
and college-type films so popular in Hollywood and appeared to ce-
ment the Marxes' reputation with film audiences around the world.
But *Duck Soup* was another story.

By 1932 the Depression had created a crisis in America. Farm
income had dropped two billion dollars, unemployment figures had
gone beyond the twelve million mark—only one in every four workers

was employed—and bank failures continued to wipe out family savings. For some reason, the Marxes and their host of writers felt the time was right to do a satire on foreign monarchies and the stupidity of war.

Getting the idea into production, however, proved to be a problem. Ever since they had come to Hollywood, the Marxes had been under the supervision of writer-producer Herman Mankiewicz (later screenwriter of *Citizen Kane* and *The Pride of the Yankees*). By nature a disorganized and excitable man, Mankiewicz felt close to the Marx style of comedy and generally let them do as they wished. For example, he agreed to the brothers' demands that they each have their own gag men, in addition to the usual screenwriters. He stood by as the traditional love story in all the musicals of the period was dropped from the Marx films in order to provide more time for the brothers' lunatic routines. But such permissiveness did not endear Mankiewicz to the big bosses at Paramount who, as mentioned in earlier chapters, were facing financial disaster in 1933. And in this struggle for survival, the Marxes found their position at the studio deteriorating day by day. Funny as they were, their last film had not made big money at the box office. Tempers flared, and finally the Marxes staged a walkout. The only person delighted with this turn of affairs was Leo McCarey, who had been ordered to direct the new Marx film. Much to his regret, peace was made between the warring parties and *Duck Soup* was readied for production. Years later, McCarey summed up the experience by saying, "The most surprising thing about this film was that I succeeded in not going crazy, for I really did not want to work with them; they were completely mad."

The clever screenplay by Bert Kalmar and Harry Ruby focused on the troubled conditions in the mythical European kingdom of Freedonia, where the wealthy Mrs. Teasdale (Dumont) handpicks Rufus T. Firefly (Groucho) as the new prime minister. Firefly's antagonist is the Sylvanian ambassador (Louis Calhern), who plots to destroy Freedonia and gain control over Mrs. Teasdale's fortune. To help him, he has hired two spies, Chicolini (Chico) and Pinkie (Harpo). Firefly's absurd policies soon engulf Freedonia in an all-out war with Sylvania and, in the end, Freedonia is victorious.

The film itself was a marvelous mixture of McCarey techniques and Marx comedy. Concerned more with spontaneity than with continuity, McCarey made a number of key contributions to the bizarre story. He cut away anything he considered unessential to the comedy itself, such as the subplots and the traditional musical numbers by Chico and Harpo. He stressed the importance of improvisation, handing Harpo a pair of scissors and telling him to cut away when the spirit moved him. Furthermore, McCarey expanded two bits of business into major comedy scenes. One was the fight between Chico and Harpo and a peanut vendor (Edgar Kennedy) outside the palace window, a scene reminiscent of the reciprocal destruction routines McCarey had helped develop in his Laurel and Hardy days. The other key routine was the classic mirror scene, in which Groucho and Harpo, dressed in identical white nightgowns, refuse to recognize the existence of each other. Despite McCarey's contributions, the Marxes still dominate the film. Their wisecracks, puns, and visual gags offer a devastating attack on patriotism, politics, government, and, most of all, war itself.

McCarey completed *Duck Soup* about the same time that the infighting at Paramount came to an end. Emmanuel Cohen emerged as the new studio head and among his first decisions were the firing of Mankiewicz and the announcement that he didn't like *Duck Soup*. He also served notice that the days of low-brow, vulgar comedy were over and that Paramount agreed with the philosophy of the new censorship code. This last pronouncement was a warning to the studio's comedians—W. C. Fields, Mae West, and the Marx Brothers —to change their ways. The Marxes seemed in the most trouble, mainly because the public agreed with Cohen in hating *Duck Soup*. Although the film died at the box office, it is considered today to be one of the Marxes' greatest works.

Zeppo felt this was a good time to leave his brothers. Never really happy with his straight-man parts, he decided to form his own talent agency. A few years later, Gummo gave up his dress business and joined him in running the agency, which remained in existence until the end of the forties. In the meantime, Groucho, Harpo, and Chico wondered what to do about their movie careers. Once more Chico came up with the answer.

Among his bridge cronies was the brilliant film producer Irving

No scene in all of the Marx Brothers' movies
has proved more popular than the "stateroom routine"
shown here from *A Night at the Opera* (1935).

Thalberg, who, along with Louis B. Mayer, had turned M-G-M into the greatest studio of its day. The only thing he had not yet done was produce a major comedy film. During the course of one of their bridge games, Chico and Thalberg discussed their mutual concerns, with the result that a business luncheon was scheduled at M-G-M for the Marxes.

The meeting proved to be a major turning point for the brothers. If they came thinking that Thalberg was going to sweet-talk them into working for M-G-M, they were wrong. Instead, the discussion centered on the trouble with the previous Marx films. Thalberg criticized their story construction, pointing out that lunatic gags didn't make for good movies or good box office. In order to be successful, he argued, comedy needed to be integrated into a well-constructed, convincing story that included a romantic subplot for the large number of women in the audience. Thalberg had two pet theories on how such a film comedy should be constructed. The first was to think of the movie as a football game. The comics should be seen as the hometown favorites playing against what appear to be unbeatable opponents. The movie, like the game, should be a series of gains and losses, with the audience rooting for its heroes. And in the end, just when it looks as if the game is lost, a miracle should occur and a last-minute touchdown win the contest. His second theory, closely linked to the football concept, was that the humor should be strung together like a clothesline. The jokes should be progressive, each one adding to the story's development and not just thrown in for the sake of comedy. In essence, Thalberg was insisting on a well-organized and carefully constructed film. At first, Groucho balked. But when he became convinced that Thalberg wasn't attacking the Marx comedy style, only its method of presentation, Groucho and his brothers agreed to move to M-G-M.

The problem of a theme for their new movie was solved one day in Thalberg's office when a screenwriter, James K. McGuinness, casually observed that "the secret of the Marx Brothers is the way they can louse up something dignified." Further discussion resulted in the world of opera being selected as the target for attack. To ensure that he would get a well-constructed story, Thalberg hired Kaufman and Morrie Ryskind to write the basic script and then added specialists in continuity and gags to rework the material.

Determined to make a success with his first comedy film, *A Night at the Opera* (1935), Thalberg suggested that the Marxes take the material on tour, testing with live audiences what was and was not funny. So, for two months, five times a day, six days a week, the Marxes, Dumont, Kitty Carlisle and Allan Jones (the love team in the film), plus four writers—Ryskind, Al Boasberg, Bob Pirosh, and George Seaton—studied audience reactions. Pirosh and Seaton even went to the trouble of timing each laugh. In this way the finished film could be edited to give time for the laughter to die down before the next gag followed. The biggest problem they encountered on tour was with the famous stateroom scene. At first, audiences didn't laugh. Then someone came up with an idea to get the laughs started. As Groucho began giving the waiter the food order, Harpo (in hiding) sounded his crazy horn to indicate one more. The repetition got audiences howling and by the end of the scene hysteria gripped the theater.

To direct the film, Thalberg selected Sam Wood, a man who had worked on one inferior movie after another since 1920. But Thalberg liked the way Wood followed orders, particularly his willingness to shoot twenty takes of each scene just so he would get a good picture. Understandably, the Marxes, who detested discipline, hated Wood, but they adored Thalberg and did whatever he asked. (Thalberg's faith in the director proved accurate, and in later years Wood turned out such memorable films as *Goodbye Mr. Chips*, *The Pride of the Yankees*, and *For Whom the Bell Tolls*.)

The film's plot illustrated Thalberg's football formula. Starting with Groucho taking advantage of Dumont's desire to enter high society, the scene quickly shifts to the backstage of the Milan Opera House where a relationship is established between the Marx Brothers and all the major characters. This, in turn, provides an opportunity for Groucho and Chico to have their famous discussion about contracts during which Groucho tries to fool Chico with his talk of a "sanity clause," and Chico responds, "You can't fool me. There ain't no sanity clause!" Confusion follows as the three Marxes now join forces to help an unknown singer win both fame and his true love against overwhelming odds. But every effort is met with failure, and just when the heroes are most depressed they try one desperate gamble which results in the most hilarious version of *Il Trovatore* ever seen on film. Of course, the gamble pays off and once more the Marxes have won the day.

Thalberg spared no expense with the production. Beautiful sets were built, lavish production numbers arranged, each scene carefully photographed, and an outstanding crew assembled. With the script's eight writers, the two months of road tests, and the Marx Brothers themselves, it seemed impossible for anything to go wrong. But the worst happened the night the finished film had its sneak preview at a local California theater. The audience hated it. Afterward, the stars were bewildered. Try as hard as they could, they just didn't under-

Although Thalberg's death took the joy out of filmmaking
for the Marx Brothers, many fans still consider *A Day at the Races* (1937)
one of the best comedies the comics ever made.
Margaret Dumont is being given the examination as a bewildered
Sig Rumann (left) and a concerned Leonard Ceeley stand helplessly by.

stand what they had done wrong. Only Thalberg kept his confidence. He felt it was a good film and a bad audience. He arranged for another sneak preview, and this time the audience loved it. The second reaction has remained true for the past forty years. Joe Adamson, the best of the Marxes' biographers, provides the reason for the film's success: "*A Night at the Opera* defines the Marx Brothers once and for all as the positive negativists in the cinema: they master one art form to demolish another, they belittle dignity so that indignities reign, and they smash the limits of good taste and proper conduct just so you won't forget their infinite, boundless personalities. The glory of this movie is that for every ounce of cynicism, there's a pound of joy."

In 1935, with their first M-G-M film a big hit, the Marxes once more thought they were on top of the world. Money, power, fame—all this was theirs—in addition to being friends with the best Hollywood producer. After a comfortable rest, they began production plans for their next M-G-M movie, *A Day at the Races*. Although not thrilled about working with director Wood again, the brothers were pleased that Pirosh and Seaton had the basic screenwriting assignment. To help the screenwriters, there was also Boasberg, who in this film provided the classic one-liner that Groucho utters while taking Harpo's pulse: "Either he's dead or my watch has stopped." After Thalberg had accepted the eighteenth draft by his writers, he sent the Marxes on tour to test the gags. Once that was finished, the film went into production. But in less than two weeks, tragedy struck.

On September 14, 1936, the frail thirty-seven-year-old Thalberg died. Plagued most of his life with poor health, the great producer refused to follow his doctor's advice that a twelve-hour day and the incredible pressure of running a major studio were too much for his weak constitution. Thalberg's death so affected the Marx Brothers personally and professionally that they were never the same again.

In addition to their love for the man, they felt that M-G-M had now set out to destroy them. By M-G-M, the Marxes meant Louis B. Mayer. Always jealous of Thalberg's talent, Mayer had a special dislike for Thalberg's friends. He felt they didn't respect him, and in the case of the Marx Brothers he was certainly right. Consider the story Groucho told of the day Mayer was having a conference with the movie censor about Lana Turner's exposing too much of her body in her last film. According to Groucho, ". . . Mayer was trying to convince the censor that M-G-M was a highly moral studio, so Harpo hired a stripper for the afternoon and chased her around the conference room."

With Thalberg gone and Mayer in complete charge, despair gripped the studio. All productions were stopped, each film resubmitted for new approval, and personnel changes made everywhere.

III

By the end of 1936 the filming of A *Day at the Races* (1937) resumed, but it seemed to lack the vitality of A *Night at the Opera*. Devoted Marx Brothers fans still enjoyed it as well as the next two M-G-M vehicles, *At the Circus* (1939) and *Go West* (1940). There are even loyal followers who find joy in *Room Service* (1938), the RKO film in which the brothers took over the parts played by other actors in a popular Broadway play. But here, too, the situations appeared routine, the comedy tired, and even fresh talent like the young Lucille Ball seemed wasted.

By 1940 the end had come not only for the Marxes but for all the fabulous talking clowns. Because the decade of the forties marks such a dramatic change in film comedy, it's important to pause briefly and consider what happened.

Some historians, like Gerald Mast, explain the decline of the personality clown by arguing that the American comic is a physical comedian and his natural medium is silence. Therefore, stars like Laurel and Hardy, W. C. Fields, Mae West, and the Marx Brothers succeeded in the thirties because the period was close enough to the silent era that they could retain their basic comic vitality. But when the complexities of sound comedy took over, the old-timers couldn't adjust and fell by the wayside. Other historians, like Donald W. McCaffrey, argue that it wasn't the complexity of sound that drove out the fabulous clowns but the change in the tastes and attitudes of a nation· facing a decade of war and despair. Even the amazing Chaplin, who didn't actually take a speaking role until his 1940 movie *The Great Dictator*, couldn't regain his hold on the audience. Instead, the public began turning to popular radio comedians like Bob Hope and Bing Crosby for the kind of light, chatty, and forgettable comedy that began in 1940 with their first picture, *Road to Singapore*, and dragged on with five more road movies until 1962, with *Road to Hong Kong*. Another theory is that the studios just didn't bother anymore with the antics of the old vaudevillians. Such talented teams as the Ritz Brothers, Abbott and Costello, the Three Stooges, Burns and Allen, and Olson and Johnson were all funny on stage and in the nightclubs, but their films were devoid of any technical skill. They appeared clever only to the very young and the very impressionable.

In 1941 the Marxes made their last significant movie, *The Big Store*. By now the brothers wanted to quit Hollywood. Groucho was the most determined. Many of his peers—Eddie Cantor, Fred Allen, Ed Wynn, Jack Benny—had moved into radio, and he wanted to join them. What's more, he had grown tired of being lumped with his brothers as great comedians. According to his son Arthur, Groucho didn't think much of his brothers' comic talents: "His evaluation of Chico was that he was a fair dialectician and a lousy pianist, and he felt that Harpo was a great pantomimist and very accomplished at the art of making faces—if one cared for that type of comedy, which he didn't." But in 1941, Chico was broke and needed money, so Groucho and Harpo agreed to do one last movie—on one condition. Chico's salary was to be turned over to them, so they could invest it for him. Reluctantly he agreed, and *The Big Store* was made. Despite its trite story about the problems of a large department store, the film has some good moments.

Afterward, the Marxes issued a statement saying that they were leaving the movies and going their own ways. Chico went back into vaudeville, playing his special brand of music. Harpo took to the stage, even playing himself in Kaufman and Moss Hart's satire on Woollcott in *The Man Who Came to Dinner*. And Groucho first tried writing and then radio. He came up with the idea for a show called "The Life of Riley," but failed in the starring role. William Bendix took it over and became a star. From time to time, the brothers got together during the war years and entertained the troops.

Unfortunately, in 1946 someone convinced them to try a movie comeback, and the result was two bad films, *A Night in Casablanca* (1946) and *Love Happy* (1949). Groucho also decided to go on his own and appeared as a solo in a series of movies best unmentioned.

Fortunately for Groucho, he also did guest bits on radio shows in the mid-forties. One show, in particular, teamed him with another guest, Bob Hope, and both comics had to wait so long for their appearance that by the time they got to the microphone they were angry. This resulted in an hilarious ad-lib session which landed Groucho an offer to emcee a new radio quiz program entitled "You Bet Your Life." Although the show got off to a rocky start when it premiered in October 1947, Groucho's ad-libbing soon caught on.

Although the Marx Brothers were never again to make great films,
there were some pretty funny gags in their romantic comedy,
At the Circus (1939). Groucho, always the big spender,
is shown courting his old flame Margaret Dumont.

Three years later "You Bet Your Life" moved over to television and enjoyed a twelve-year run.

In 1973 the Motion Picture Academy decided to award a special citation to the Marx Brothers. Of the famous trio, only Groucho was alive. Chico had died on October 11, 1961; Harpo on September 28, 1964. To coincide with the Academy Award, a local Los Angeles television station began rerunning tapes of the old "You Bet Your Life" shows, and the idea proved so successful that the series is more popular in the mid-seventies than in the fifties.

Reading about the Marxes today, one finds all sorts of reasons for their popularity. Some say it's because of the nostalgia craze, others claim that there are no new clowns around, and still others say it's just curiosity. But for me, critic Allen Eyles summed up the answer best when he wrote, "Perhaps the Marxes' finest quality is their underlying purity or innocence. They have no permanent truck with this base world of ours, full of menial considerations, dull routines, and comfortable conformism. . . . They oppose education, culture, and all forms of regulation as destroying the natural life and man's innate dignity."

EPILOGUE

The decline of the great personality clowns, which began in the late 1930s, has persisted until very recently. The story of their rise and fall helps illustrate the changes that took place in the film industry, as well as in film audiences, from 1927 to the late 1960s. In the early days of the talkies, there were still artists and producers able and willing to criticize social conditions. They loved being subversive. They delighted in challenging viewers to reevaluate society's values. But as the 1940s approached, censors and tastemakers felt the critical comedians had gone too far. The studios agreed. Before long, no one seemed interested in the great clowns. In their place came new faces like Bob Hope, Danny Kaye, Jack Benny, Red Skelton, Bud Abbott, Lou Costello, and Jerry Lewis. These lesser comedians emphasized sentimental humor. A wisecrack here and there about morality and values, but always careful to offend no one. The end result was to reinforce conventional standards. This became the norm for close to twenty-five years.

The history of great personality clowns, thankfully, does not end with the 1930s. Today the public has once more warmed to attacks on conventional morality. Audiences everywhere applaud laughmakers who challenge existing social conditions. As a result, the times have produced such first-rate comedians as Woody Allen, Jack Lemmon, Mel Brooks, Barbra Streisand, Gene Wilder, and Madeline Kahn. It's easier now to understand the appeal of the first talking clowns. By discovering what these famous comedians were like, we should be better able to understand how they related both to their times and to ours. In our present state of unrest and frustration, we benefit from watching their movies. We discover that while our problems may change with the times, they are never solved. Great comedy teaches us to live with ourselves and our world, for better or worse.

We can be grateful that these marvelous comedians remain like brave warriors in the cause of laughter and refuse to pass away.

BIBLIOGRAPHY

The author hopes that the following selective book list will help the interested reader to explore more fully the history of the sound comedians. Because of this book's brevity, only a few writers' opinions were singled out, and for that reason extensive references to specific authors are rarely given. Anyone reading the following publications, which the author has consulted, will have no difficulty in determining which portions were made use of.

GENERAL REFERENCES

Durgnat, Raymond. *The Crazy Mirror: Hollywood Comedy and the American Image*. New York: Horizon Press, 1970.

Maltin, Leonard. *Movie Comedy Teams*. New York: Signet, 1970.

Manchel, Frank. *Yesterday's Clowns: The Rise of Film Comedy*. New York: Franklin Watts, Inc., 1973.

Mast, Gerald. *The Comic Mind: Comedy and the Movies*. New York: The Bobbs-Merrill Company, Inc., 1973.

McCaffrey, Donald W. *The Golden Age of Sound Comedy: Comic Films and Comedians of the Thirties*. New York: A. S. Barnes & Company, 1973.

I. THE IMMORTAL BRATS: STAN LAUREL AND OLIVER HARDY

Barr, Charles. *Laurel and Hardy*. Berkeley: University of California Press, 1968.

Everson, William K. "The Crazy World of Laurel and Hardy," *Take One* 1:9 (1968), 16–19.

——. *The Films of Hal Roach*. New York: The Museum of Modern Art, 1971.

——. *The Films of Laurel and Hardy*. New York: The Citadel Press, 1967.

—— (editor). *The Laurel and Hardy Book*. New York: Curtis Books, 1973.

McCabe, John. *The Comedy World of Stan Laurel*. New York: Doubleday & Co., Inc., 1974.

——. *Mr. Laurel and Mr. Hardy*. New York: Grosset and Dunlap, 1966.

Robinson, David. "The Lighter People," *Sight and Sound* 24:1 (July–September 1954), 39–42, 52.

Spensley, Dorothy. "Those Two Goofy Guys," *Photoplay* 38:2 (July 1930), 72, 136.

Thompson, Howard. "Hal Roach's Laugh Factory," *The New York Times* (July 11, 1965) x5.

Verb, Boyd. "Laurel Without Hardy," *Films in Review* 10:3 (March 1959), 153–58.

II. THE NOBLEST FRAUD: W. C. FIELDS

Bergman, Andrew. *We're in the Money: Depression America and its Films*. New York: Harper and Row, 1971.

Cary, Harold. "The Loneliest Man in the Movies," *Colliers* 76 (November 28, 1925), 26.

Deschner, Donald. *The Films of W. C. Fields*. New York: The Citadel Press, 1966.

Everson, William K. *The Art of W. C. Fields*. New York: Bonanza Books, 1967.

Fields, Ronald J. *W. C. Fields by Himself: His Intended Autobiography*. Englewood Cliffs: Prentice-Hall, Inc., 1973.

Fields, W. C. *Screenplay of "The Bank Dick."* New York: Simon and Schuster, 1973.

————. *Screenplay of "Never Give a Sucker an Even Break" and "Tillie and Gus."* New York: Simon and Schuster, 1973.

Fowler, Gene. *Minutes of the Last Meeting*. New York: The Viking Press, 1954.

Johnston, Alva. "Who Knows What Is Funny?" *The Saturday Evening Post* 211 (August 6, 1938), 10–11, 43, 45–46.

Markfield, Wallace. "The Dark Geography of W. C. Fields," *The New York Times Magazine* (April 24, 1966), 32–33, 110, 112, 116, 119, 120.

Monti, Carlotta, with Rice, Cy. *W. C. Fields and Me*. Englewood Cliffs: Prentice-Hall, Inc., 1971.

Robinson, David. "Dukenfield Meets McCargle: Creation of a Character," *Sight and Sound* 36:3 (Summer, 1967) 125–29.

Taylor, Robert Lewis. *W. C. Fields: His Fortunes and Follies*. New York: Doubleday & Company, Inc. 1949.

Tynan, Ken. "Toby Jug and Bottle," *Sight and Sound* 19:10 (February, 1951), 395–98.

Wilson, Robert (editor). *The Film Criticism of Otis Ferguson*. Philadelphia: Temple University Press, 1971.

Yanni, Nicholas. *W. C. Fields*. New York: Pyramid Publications, 1974.

III. THE FUNNIEST BAD GIRL: MAE WEST

Condon, Frank. "Come Up and Meet Mae West," *Collier's* 93:24 (June 16, 1934), 26, 42.

Haskall, Molly. *From Reverance to Rape: The Treatment of Women in Film*. New York: Holt, Rinehart and Winston, 1974.

Jennings, C. R. "Playboy Interview: Mae West," *Playboy* 18:11 (January, 1971), 73–82.

Knight, Arthur, and Alpert, Hollis. *The History of Sex in the Cinema*. Chicago: Playboy Press, 1965.

Mayer, Arthur. *Merely Colossal: The Story of the Movies from the Long Chase to the Chaise Longue*. New York: Simon and Schuster, 1953.

Mellen, Joan. *Women and Their Sexuality in the New Film*. New York: Horizon Press, 1973.

Parish, James Robert, with Whitney, Steven. *The George Raft File: The Unauthorized Biography*. New York: Drake Publishers, Inc., 1973.

Ringgold, Gene. "Mae West," *Screen Facts* 2:1 (1964), 1–24.

Roberts, Steven V. "76—And Still Diamond Lil," *The New York Times Magazine,* (November 2, 1969), 64–65, 67, 70, 72, 74, 77, 80, 82.
Tuska, Jon. *The Films of Mae West.* Secaucus, N. J.: The Citadel Press, 1973.
Weintraub, Joseph (editor). *The Wit and Wisdom of Mae West.* New York: G. P. Putnam's Sons, 1967.
West, Mae. *Goodness Had Nothing to Do With It.* Enlarged and Revised. New York: Macfadden-Bartell Corporation, 1970.
Yablonsky, Lewis. *George Raft.* New York: McGraw-Hill Book Company, 1974.
Zukor, Adolph, with Kramer, Dale. *The Public Is Never Wrong.* New York: G. P. Putnam's Sons, 1953.

IV. THE LUNATIC CLOWNS: THE MARX BROTHERS

Adamson, Joe. *Groucho, Harpo, Chico—and Sometimes Zeppo: A Celebration of the Marx Brothers.* New York: Simon and Schuster, 1973.
Anobile, Richard J. (editor). *Hooray for Captain Spaulding!: Visual and Verbal Gems from "Animal Crackers."* New York: Darien House, Inc., 1974.
———. *Why a Duck?* New York: Darien House, Inc., 1971.
Chandler, Charlotte: "Playboy Interview: Groucho Marx," *Playboy* (October 1973), 59–60, 66, 69, 72, 74, 185–86.
Classic Film Scripts: The Four Marx Brothers in "Monkey Business" and "Duck Soup." New York: Simon and Schuster, 1973.
Crichton, Kyle. *The Marx Brothers.* Garden City, New York: Doubleday & Co., Inc., 1950.
Daney, Serge Daney, and Noames, Jean-Louis. "Taking Chances: Interview with Leo McCarey," *Cahiers du Cinema in English* 7 (January 1967), 42–54.
Eyles, Allen. *The Marx Brothers and Their World of Comedy.* New York: A. S. Barnes and Company, 1966.
Marx, Arthur. *Life With a Groucho.* New York: Simon and Schuster, 1954.
———. *Son of Groucho.* New York: David McKay Company, Inc., 1972.
Marx, Groucho. *Groucho and Me.* New York: Bernard Geis Associates, 1959.
———, and Anobile, Richard J. *The Marx Bros. Scrapbook.* New York: Darien House, Inc., 1973.
Marx, Harpo. "My Brother Groucho," *Coronet* 29 (February 1951), 130–35.
———, with Barber, Rowland. *Harpo Speaks!* New York: Bernard Geis Associates, 1961.
Meredith, Scott. *George S. Kaufman and His Friends.* Garden City, New York: Doubleday & Co., Inc., 1974.
A Night at the Opera: Story by James Kevin McGuinness: Screenplay by George S. Kaufman and Morrie Ryskind. New York: The Viking Press, 1972.
Zimmerman, Paul D., and Golblatt, Burt. *The Marx Brothers at the Movies* New York, G. P. Putnam's Sons, 1968.

INDEX

791.43028
M   Manchel, F.   c. 1

        The talking clowns

		DATE DUE	